Reader's Digest
Pathfinders

Rocks and Minerals

A Reader's Digest Pathfinder

Reader's Digest Children's Books are published by
Reader's Digest Children's Publishing, Inc.
Reader's Digest Road, Pleasantville, NY, 10570-7000, U.S.A.

Conceived and produced by Weldon Owen Pty Limited
59 Victoria Street, McMahons Point, NSW, 2060, Australia
A member of the Weldon Owen Group of Companies
Sydney • San Francisco

© 1999 Weldon Owen Inc.

READER'S DIGEST CHILDREN'S PUBLISHING, INC.
Senior Project Editors: Sherry Gerstein, Beverly Larson
Associate Editor: Dina Rubin
Assistant Editor: Lori Froeb
Project Creative Director: Candy Warren
Art Director: Fredric Winkowski
Production Coordinator: Debbie Gagnon

WELDON OWEN PTY LTD
Chairman: John Owen
Publisher: Sheena Coupe
Associate Publisher: Lynn Humphries
Art Director: Sue Burk
Consultant, Design Concept and Cover Design: John Bull
Design Concept: Clare Forte, Robyn Latimer
Editorial Assistants: Sarah Anderson, Trudie Craig
Production Manager: Caroline Webber
Production Assistant: James Blackman
Vice President International Sales: Stuart Laurence

Author: Tracy Staedter
Consultants: Robert Coenraads, Ph.D., Carolyn Rebbert, Ph.D.
Project Editor: Scott Forbes
Designer: Cathy Campbell
Picture Research: Debra Wager

Illustrators: Andrew Beckett/Illustration, Chris Forsey,
Ray Grinaway, David McAllister, Stuart McVicar, Michael Saunders,
Kevin Stead, Sharif Tarabay/Illustration, Thomas Trojer

Library of Congress Cataloging–in–Publication Data

Staedter, Tracy.
Rocks and minerals / [Tracy Staedter, author].
p.   cm. — (Reader's Digest pathfinders)
Includes index.
Summary: Examines the nature, formation, and different kinds of rocks and minerals
and explains how to collect them.
ISBN 0-7944-0372-7 paperback.
1. Rocks—Juvenile literature. 2. Minerals—Juvenile literature.
[1. Rocks. 2. Minerals.] I. Title. II. Series.
QE432.2.S73   1999   552—dc21   98-53125

Color Reproduction by Colourscan Co Pte Ltd
Printed by Tien Wah Press Pte Ltd
Printed in Singapore

A WELDON OWEN PRODUCTION

Reader's Digest
Pathfinders

Rocks and
Minerals

Reader's Digest

Children's Books™

Pleasantville, New York • Montréal, Québec

Contents

Pick Your Path!

ROCKS AND MINERALS is different from any other information book you've ever picked up. You can start at the beginning and learn about our rocky planet, then read through to the end and find out how to collect rocks and minerals. Or, if you have a special interest in crystals, jump right into the "Meet the Minerals" section and move through the book from there.

You'll find plenty of other discovery paths to choose from in the special features sections. Read about big discoveries and the scientists who made them in "Inside Story," or get creative with "Hands On" activities. Delve into words with "Word Builders," or amaze your friends with fascinating facts from "That's Amazing!" You can choose a new path with every reading—READER'S DIGEST PATHFINDERS will take you wherever *you* want to go.

INSIDE STORY
Great Moments in Geology

Investigate the spectacular canyons of the southwestern United States with explorer John Wesley Powell. Go rock hunting on the Moon with geologist Harrison Schmitt. Read photographer Brad Lewis's account of what it's like to have a volcano in your backyard. Read about great scientists and geology's historic events in INSIDE STORY. Imagine that you are there behind the scenes, and you will understand how it feels to witness or do something that changes the world.

HANDS ON
Create and Make

Squeeze a sugar cube and watch it glow in the dark. Fold layers of modeling clay into mountain ranges. Create seismic waves in a bowl of water. Grow your own crystals in a jar. Construct a simple display case for your rock and mineral collection. Learn how to identify minerals by examining their density, color, and hardness. The HANDS ON features showcase experiments, projects, and activities—each one related to that page's main subject.

Word Builders

What a strange word! What does it mean? Where did it come from? Find out by reading *Word Builders*.

That's Amazing!

Awesome facts, amazing records, fascinating figures— you'll find them all in *That's Amazing!*

Pathfinder

Use the *Pathfinder* section to find your way from one subject to another. It's all up to you.

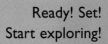

Ready! Set! Start exploring!

Rocks

YOU ARE STANDING on an enormous rock. This rock is hurtling through space. Our planet, Earth, is a giant ball of rock—actually, many different kinds of rocks. These rocks are, in turn, made of minerals, which are naturally formed solids. You may not notice, but rocks are always changing. Hot, liquid rock—buoyed by heat from Earth's core—rises to the surface, where it cools and hardens. Ice, wind, and water constantly break down surface rocks into pieces. Rocks sink beneath the crust and melt again. This cycle, which has been going on for billions of years, creates three main kinds of rock—igneous, sedimentary, and metamorphic.

Rocks Around the Clock

STEP OUTSIDE, and you'll be surrounded—by rocks. Look down. Under the soil, the ground is made of many kinds of rock. Look up. Gigantic boulders and jagged slabs of stone make up hills and mountains. Some rocks formed just days ago. Some have been here for billions of years.

Pick up a rock and feel its weight. Ancient people noticed that rocks were tough as well, so they used them to build houses and roads. They also realized that some rocks contained useful minerals such as metals, which they soon learned to separate from rocks. Today we still process rocks. We extract metals used in bridges, cars, and skyscrapers. We crush rock to make railroad beds and to produce construction materials for buildings. We even extract the fuel to power trucks or heat our homes from rock layers below the ground.

We depend on rocks and minerals all day long. Faucets and water pipes are made of metals. The wires that carry electricity are made of copper, which is also a metal. We eat with metal utensils and flavor our food with rock crystals called salt. We write with pencils that contain a black mineral called graphite. Our computers wouldn't work without the crystals of quartz used to make silicon chips. Even plastic objects such as bottles and bowls are made with oil from rocks. Just where would we be without rocks and minerals?

A ROCKY LANDSCAPE

Rocks give shape to the land around us. You can see this most clearly on mountain peaks, streambeds, coastlines, and some roadways. Humans collect rocks from mines and quarries, using them to make buildings and machines, and turning them into all kinds of products from jewels to fuel.

The land around us is all rock. You can see this most clearly on mountain peaks and at coastal cliffs.

Most modern buildings are made of steel, concrete, and glass, all of which come from rocks.

HANDS ON

Rock Spotting

❶ Find a notebook and pen and take a look around your house. Make a list of all the things that you think are made of rocks and minerals. (The pictures at the top and bottom of this page will help you out.) Then go for a walk around your neighborhood. Again, try to guess which objects are made of rocks and minerals, and write them down in another list.

❷ Now, put your lists away for a while. When you finish reading this book, try the exercise again and make new lists. You'll be amazed how many more objects made from rocks and minerals you recognize.

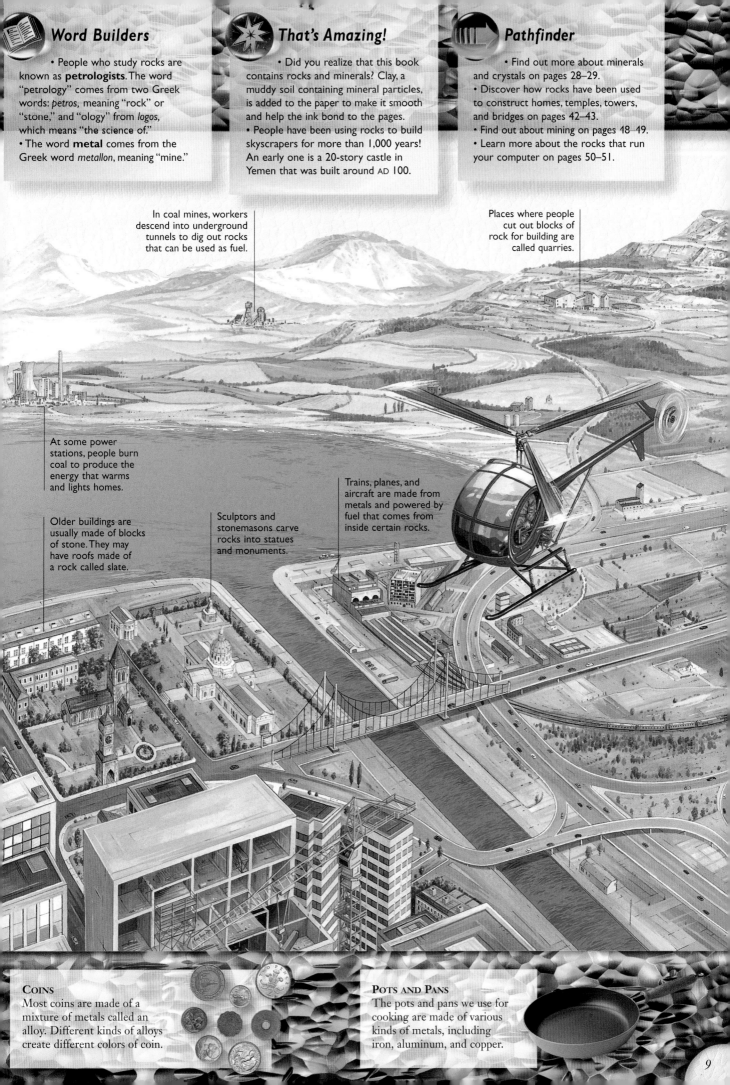

Word Builders

- People who study rocks are known as **petrologists**. The word "petrology" comes from two Greek words: *petros,* meaning "rock" or "stone," and "ology" from *logos,* which means "the science of."
- The word **metal** comes from the Greek word *metallon,* meaning "mine."

That's Amazing!

- Did you realize that this book contains rocks and minerals? Clay, a muddy soil containing mineral particles, is added to the paper to make it smooth and help the ink bond to the pages.
- People have been using rocks to build skyscrapers for more than 1,000 years! An early one is a 20-story castle in Yemen that was built around AD 100.

Pathfinder

- Find out more about minerals and crystals on pages 28–29.
- Discover how rocks have been used to construct homes, temples, towers, and bridges on pages 42–43.
- Find out about mining on pages 18–19.
- Learn more about the rocks that run your computer on pages 50–51.

In coal mines, workers descend into underground tunnels to dig out rocks that can be used as fuel.

Places where people cut out blocks of rock for building are called quarries.

At some power stations, people burn coal to produce the energy that warms and lights homes.

Older buildings are usually made of blocks of stone. They may have roofs made of a rock called slate.

Sculptors and stonemasons carve rocks into statues and monuments.

Trains, planes, and aircraft are made from metals and powered by fuel that comes from inside certain rocks.

COINS
Most coins are made of a mixture of metals called an alloy. Different kinds of alloys create different colors of coin.

POTS AND PANS
The pots and pans we use for cooking are made of various kinds of metals, including iron, aluminum, and copper.

Third Rock from the Sun

OUR PLANET is just one of many large rocks that travel around a star we call the Sun. Planets, moons, asteroids, meteoroids, and comets all share our part of the universe. Together, these rocks form a cosmic community called the solar system. Earth's address in the solar system is planet number 3, or third rock from the Sun.

Earth and the rest of the solar system formed about five billion years ago from a cloud of dust, rocks, and gas. These materials whirled around the Sun, continually crashing into each other. Some of the rock fragments stuck together, eventually forming a number of planets, including Earth. Earth's early history was like a demolition derby, with comets and asteroids constantly smashing into the new planet. All of these collisions plus decaying radioactive minerals created intense heat inside Earth and on its surface.

All of this heat had a profound effect on young Earth. Material inside began to melt. The heaviest parts sank to the core. The lighter substances floated up and formed the crust. Other matter settled in layers in between. We can't see these layers, but we can detect them. Scientists use instruments called geophones to listen to Earth's insides, just as a doctor uses a stethoscope to listen to your heart. This has allowed scientists to identify several layers. If we could slice the planet in half, these layers would look like the rings around a bull's-eye.

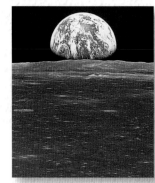

MOON WITH A VIEW
Earth looks like a giant blue marble when seen from its neighbor, the Moon. Many scientists believe that the Moon formed billions of years ago when a small planet smashed into Earth and pieces of debris from the collision stuck together.

Continental crust: 12–43 miles (20–70 km) thick

Ocean crust: 3 miles (5 km) thick

Upper mantle: 434 miles (700 km) thick

	Mantle	Outer core	Inner core
	1,800 miles (2,900 km) thick	1,400 miles (2,250 km) thick	750 miles (1,200 km) thick

HANDS ON

Making Waves

To learn about Earth's interior, seismologists study seismic waves—waves from earthquakes or underground explosions that the scientists set off—as they travel through the planet. By measuring how fast and in which direction the waves move, the scientists can tell what kinds of rocks are present and how thick they are. In this project, the waves act like seismic waves, and the water and bottle act like rock layers.

❶ Fill a large bowl with water, then place a bottle in the middle of the bowl.

❷ Gently pour some drops of water into the side of the bowl. Ripples will move outward from the point where the drops hit the water. When the ripples hit the bottle, they are deflected. In the same way, seismic waves are deflected by certain kinds of rock.

Word Builders

• The word **gravity** comes from the Latin *gravitas*, meaning "heaviness."
• Waves from underground explosions are called **seismic waves**, and people who study these waves are called **seismologists**. The words come from the Greek *seismos*, meaning "earthquake."

That's Amazing!

• Digging at a rate of one foot (30 cm) per minute, it would take you 87 years to tunnel through Earth.
• The world's deepest drill hole, at Zapolyarnyy in eastern Russia, is nine miles (15 km) deep. However, this is barely a scratch on Earth's surface.

Pathfinder

• Hot rocks in the mantle rise as cooler rocks sink. This creates convection currents which in turn cause earthquakes and volcanoes. Find out how this happens on pages 12–13.
• Earth's rocky surface is shaped by forces called weathering and erosion. Turn to pages 14–15.
• When meteoroids crash to Earth, they are called meteorites. Take a look at a couple of meteorites on pages 24–25.

INSIDE STORY
Journey to the Center of the Earth

More than one hundred years ago, a French writer named Jules Verne took his readers to the center of our planet. In his book *A Journey to the Center of the Earth*, written in 1864 (and later made into a film), he described a route from one side of Earth to the other, through dark passages and past underground waterfalls, stony towers, and rivers of molten rock. We now know that this journey would be impossible, but explorations have shown that Verne's descriptions were like the extraordinary world of underground caves—a world he had never seen.

Asthenosphere

Lithosphere (crust plus upper mantle)

MAKING A SOLAR SYSTEM

The solar system is our cosmic home. Like all homes, it is made up of scraps of different materials. But the solar system wasn't built with lumber and nails. Instead, it came together from dust and gas.

About five billion years ago, a slowly spinning cloud of dust and hot gas—called a nebula—began to shrink. As it shrank, it spun faster and faster.

UPPER CRUST
Satellite photos allow us to study Earth's rocky surface. This picture shows the Himalaya Mountains in Asia.

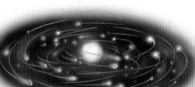

Hot gases at the center were pulled together, forming the Sun. Cooler gases and dust at the edges began to cluster, forming huge chunks of space rubble.

WHAT'S INSIDE?
Earth is made up of several layers. The ground you stand on (the crust) and the rock beneath it (the upper mantle) form a layer called the lithosphere. The lithosphere rides on a layer of partially molten rock called the asthenosphere, which is in the upper part of a larger layer called the mantle. Beneath the mantle lie a liquid outer core and a solid inner core of iron and nickel.

After 100 million years or so, nine of these big chunks were left spinning around the Sun. These formed the planets we know today.

Uranus   *Neptune*   • *Pluto*

Mount Everest,
Nepal

Klyuchevskaya
volcano, Russia

Sugarloaf Mountain,
Brazil

Restless Earth

AT THE CENTER of Earth lies a tremendous powerhouse. It is a blistering hot core of iron and nickel. The energy generated here is so mighty that it fuels violent events on Earth's surface, more than 1,800 miles (2,900 km) away. Heat from the core bakes the rock directly above it, in the mantle. As the mantle cooks, hot rocks rise like bubbles in boiling water. The cooler parts of the mantle sink, but they are reheated by the core and soon rise again. This constant cycle of rising and sinking forms convection currents.

As rock circulates in a convection current, it pushes and tugs at Earth's crust. Shortly after Earth formed, these movements cracked the lithosphere, turning it into a global jigsaw puzzle. The pieces of the puzzle are known as tectonic plates, and they float on top of the asthenosphere, carrying the world's oceans and landmasses.

When molten rock oozes up between two plates, the plates move away from each other. But the plates can travel only so far before they crash into other plates. If you live near the edge of a plate, you can feel the effects of these collisions when earthquakes rumble. You can also see the effects when volcanoes erupt. Over time, these violent episodes slowly reshape the face of our planet.

KOBE QUAKE
In 1995, a massive earthquake rattled the city of Kobe in Japan, toppling buildings and freeways like playing cards. More than 5,000 people died, and tens of thousands lost their homes.

THE SHIFTING SURFACE
Convection currents (indicated by red arrows below) stretch and squeeze the crust. Where plates separate, ocean ridges and rift valleys appear. Where plates smash into each other, mountains, volcanoes, and undersea valleys form.

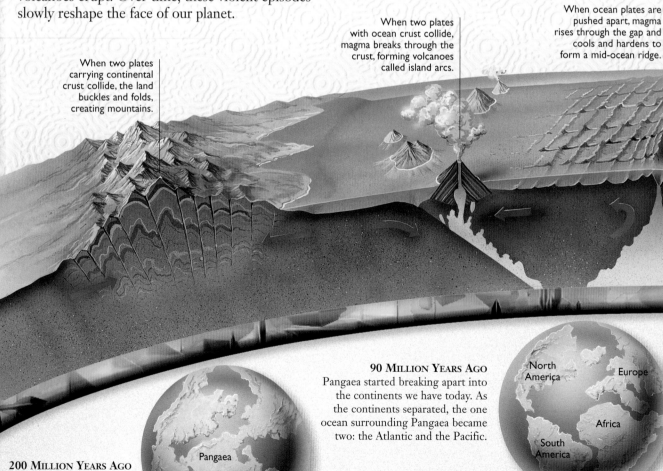

When two plates carrying continental crust collide, the land buckles and folds, creating mountains.

When two plates with ocean crust collide, magma breaks through the crust, forming volcanoes called island arcs.

When ocean plates are pushed apart, magma rises through the gap and cools and hardens to form a mid-ocean ridge.

90 MILLION YEARS AGO
Pangaea started breaking apart into the continents we have today. As the continents separated, the one ocean surrounding Pangaea became two: the Atlantic and the Pacific.

North America

Europe

Africa

South America

Pangaea

200 MILLION YEARS AGO
The world's landmasses were clustered together, forming one enormous continent called Pangaea, and surrounded by one large ocean.

CONTINENTS ON THE MOVE

For millions of years, the movements of Earth's plates have been shrinking and enlarging oceans, and splitting and joining continents.

Word Builders

- The word **volcano** comes from the name of the Roman god of fire and metalworking, Vulcan. He was said to live beneath a volcano on the present-day island of Vulcano in Italy.
- **Pangaea** is the name of the single continent that existed 200 million years ago. Pangaea comes from the Greek words for "all of Earth."

That's Amazing!

- About 800 strong earthquakes shake the planet each year, but about 8,000 minor ones happen every day. Fortunately, these minor quakes are too weak to cause any damage.
- The plates surrounding the Pacific Ocean are colliding with ocean crust, forming an almost complete circle of volcanoes known as the Ring of Fire.

Pathfinder

- Lava cools and hardens to form various kinds of rocks. Learn about volcanic rocks on pages 18–19.
- When plate movements squeeze or heat Earth's crust, some rocks change into different rocks. Find out how this happens on pages 22–23.
- Discover how scientists study and map the ocean floor on pages 46–47.

INSIDE STORY

A Volcano in My Yard

Brad Lewis lives on a volcano. He makes his home in Pahoa, Hawaii, on the northeast side of Kilauea, a highly active hot-spot volcano. "Last night I saw a giant river of lava pumping into the ocean," he says. Brad works as a photographer, so he took pictures of the event. Because seawater cools and hardens molten rock, Brad was witnessing the birth of new land. Over the years, he has seen beaches grow and bays turn into peninsulas. Brad enjoys living on Hawaii. He says the volcano keeps him humble by reminding him that "Earth has its own plans."

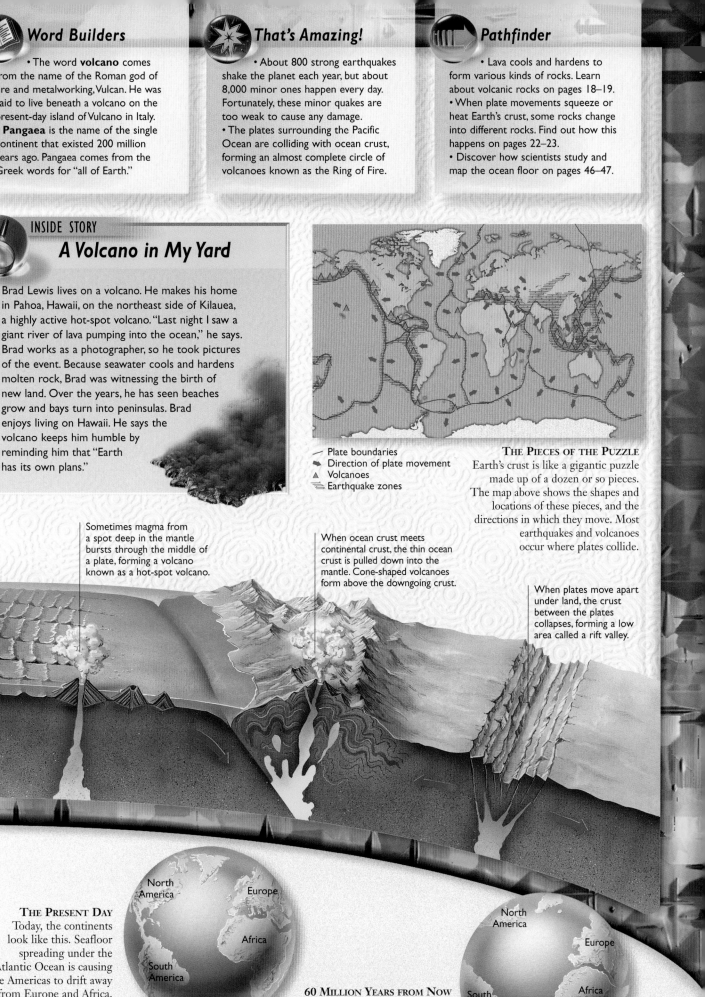

⌐ Plate boundaries
◣ Direction of plate movement
▲ Volcanoes
≋ Earthquake zones

THE PIECES OF THE PUZZLE
Earth's crust is like a gigantic puzzle made up of a dozen or so pieces. The map above shows the shapes and locations of these pieces, and the directions in which they move. Most earthquakes and volcanoes occur where plates collide.

Sometimes magma from a spot deep in the mantle bursts through the middle of a plate, forming a volcano known as a hot-spot volcano.

When ocean crust meets continental crust, the thin ocean crust is pulled down into the mantle. Cone-shaped volcanoes form above the downgoing crust.

When plates move apart under land, the crust between the plates collapses, forming a low area called a rift valley.

THE PRESENT DAY
Today, the continents look like this. Seafloor spreading under the Atlantic Ocean is causing the Americas to drift away from Europe and Africa.

North America
Europe
Africa
South America

60 MILLION YEARS FROM NOW
The Atlantic Ocean might continue to widen. New continents will form as more plate collisions occur.

North America
Europe
Africa
South America

Delicate Arch,
United States

Tasman Glacier,
New Zealand

Numbung Pinnacles,
Australia

Wear and Tear

OUR PLANET cannot protect itself from harsh weather as you do. You can put on a coat when the day grows cold. You can open an umbrella to stay dry when it rains. But not Earth. It cannot escape the snow, ice, heat, pollution, wind, or rain. It is constantly being soaked and dried out, frozen and burned.

Just as heat, wind, and cold dry out and crack your skin, so these natural elements cause Earth's rocks to split and crumble. Rocks are also eaten away by chemicals in rainwater and broken up by the movement of plant roots. These processes are known as weathering. Glaciers, streams, oceans, and wind transport rock fragments over exposed rocks, scouring and carving their surfaces, and depositing the fragments in rivers, oceans, and lakes. This is called erosion.

As weathering and erosion sculpt the landscape, they create features such as caves, canyons, sea stacks, and jagged mountain peaks. Where hard rock resists the elements, unusual rock formations such as mesas, arches, and pinnacles may occur. But no rock holds out forever. Over time, cliffs crumble, mountains shrink, and coastlines wear away.

GLACIAL EROSION
Glaciers are nature's bulldozers. These massive slabs of ice form on mountains, then slowly slide downhill, gouging out valleys as easily as you can scoop up dirt with your hand.

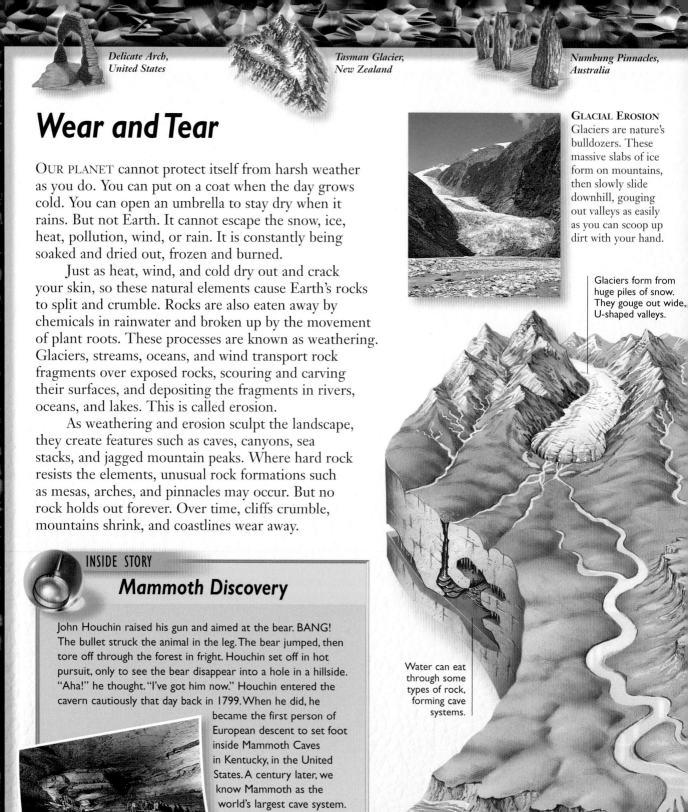

Glaciers form from huge piles of snow. They gouge out wide, U-shaped valleys.

Water can eat through some types of rock, forming cave systems.

The ocean waves pound shorelines, cutting sea caves and columns called stacks.

INSIDE STORY
Mammoth Discovery

John Houchin raised his gun and aimed at the bear. BANG! The bullet struck the animal in the leg. The bear jumped, then tore off through the forest in fright. Houchin set off in hot pursuit, only to see the bear disappear into a hole in a hillside. "Aha!" he thought. "I've got him now." Houchin entered the cavern cautiously that day back in 1799. When he did, he became the first person of European descent to set foot inside Mammoth Caves in Kentucky, in the United States. A century later, we know Mammoth as the world's largest cave system. But no one knows what happened to the bear.

NATURE'S SCULPTORS
From mountain peaks to underground caves, and from deserts to seashores, the forces of nature create an incredible variety of landscapes.

Word Builders

- The word **glacier** comes from the French word *glace,* meaning "ice."
- **Mesas** are flat-topped, steep-sided landforms. Mesa is a Spanish word that comes from the Latin *mensa,* meaning "table." Small mesas are called **buttes**. Butte comes from an old French word *bute,* meaning "mound" or "hill."

That's Amazing!

- The world's largest single cave is Sarawak Chamber in Borneo, Malaysia. It is big enough to hold eight jumbo jets.
- At any time, the world's rivers contain 302 cubic miles (1,260 cubic km) of water. If rain stopped falling and the rivers dried up, the sea would evaporate at a rate of 3 feet (1 m) each year.

Pathfinder

- Erosion is part of a process that continually recycles rocks. Read about this process on pages 16–17.
- Rock fragments deposited by rivers may eventually cement together to form new rock. Find out how on pages 20–21.
- Curious about canyons? Take a look inside the biggest canyon in the world on pages 46–47.
- Learn more about erosion at the seashore on pages 58–59.

HANDS ON

Cracking Up

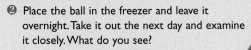

1. Roll a piece of modeling clay into a round ball. Wet it and then cover it with plastic wrap.

2. Place the ball in the freezer and leave it overnight. Take it out the next day and examine it closely. What do you see?

3. Cracks will have formed in the clay. This is because the water expands when it freezes, splitting the clay. The same thing happens to rock when it freezes.

Rivers carve canyons and mesas, and wash away rocks and dirt.

ONION-SKIN WEATHERING
A constant cycle of soaking, drying, freezing, and thawing has caused these huge boulders in central Australia to crack and peel. The rock comes off in layers—just like the skin of an onion.

In deserts, wind-blown sand wears away rock and forms shifting dunes.

ROCK PINNACLES
At Bryce Canyon in the United States, weathering and erosion have shaped the stone into spires called hoodoos.

HOODOOS

The rocks of Bryce Canyon in Utah, U.S.A., formed at the bottom of a lake 50–60 million years ago. Since then, nature has been hard at work, sculpting strange stone columns known as hoodoos.

Small cracks crisscross the rock in the hillside. Water flowing down the hill cuts into the cracks, forming deep, narrow gullies. The water also seeps into cracks in the walls of the gullies.

In winter, the water freezes and expands, widening the cracks in the walls. Slowly, stone columns emerge. Because some types of rock erode more quickly than others, the columns form strange shapes.

Some of the columns topple or crumble to dust. Eventually, this set of hoodoos will disappear. But new ones will already be forming in the hillside.

The Rock Cycle

YOU WON'T NOTICE THIS, but the rocks around you are on a slow-motion roller coaster. Geological forces thrust them up as mountains, spew them into the air as molten rock, break them into bits and pieces, and plunge them deep under ground. Gradually, this rocky ride turns our planet almost completely inside out. Peaks become valleys, and ocean floors turn into mountains, leaving the remains of sea creatures on top of towering peaks such as the Himalayas in Asia.

During this turbulent ride, three different kinds of rock appear. When molten rock cools, igneous rocks form. When rocks on Earth's surface are pummeled to pieces by waves, broken up by ice, or scoured to bits by other rocks, the fragments settle in layers and become sedimentary rocks. Meanwhile, deep inside Earth, fierce temperatures and intense pressure cook and squeeze rocks, transforming them into metamorphic rocks.

It wasn't until this century that scientists figured out how long this roller coaster has been running. We now know it began when Earth formed, nearly five billion years ago. By our standards, the ride is a slow one. But for a rock, it's a journey that repeats over and over.

NEW ROCK FROM UNDER THE SEA
In 1963, an undersea volcano near Iceland gave birth to an island, Surtsey. Soon, plants and animals colonized the new land.

Molten rock cools and hardens to form igneous rocks.

Heat and pressure under ground create metamorphic rocks.

HANDS ON

Geologic Time

Geologists divide Earth's history into eras, which are shown in the diagram below. To understand the history of human life relative to the age of Earth, try this. Stand with your arms stretched out. Imagine that the span of your arms represents the entire history of our planet. The tip of the middle finger of your right hand is when Earth formed. The first era—the Precambrian or Cryptozoic—stretches all the way from the tip of your right hand to your left wrist (A).
The first plants emerge at the bottom of your palm (B). Dinosaurs appear at the bottom of your middle finger (C), then vanish suddenly at the finger's top joint (D). The entire history of the human race perches on the middle fingertip of your left hand (E).

A B CDE

First insects

First land plants

First fish

Silurian   Devonian

Ordovician   410 mya   360 mya

435 mya Glaciers on most continents

Cambrian   500 mya

Many new life forms emerge

First small, shelly animals

570 mya

Earliest glaciation   1 bya Blue-green bacteria form large reefs

First soft-bodied animals

2.5 bya 75% of continents formed

2 bya Oxygen-producing bacteria abundant

Earth begins to form   Atmosphere begins to form

Earth's crust begins to form   3 bya Oldest known rocks form   Abundant surface water

4 bya

4.5 bya

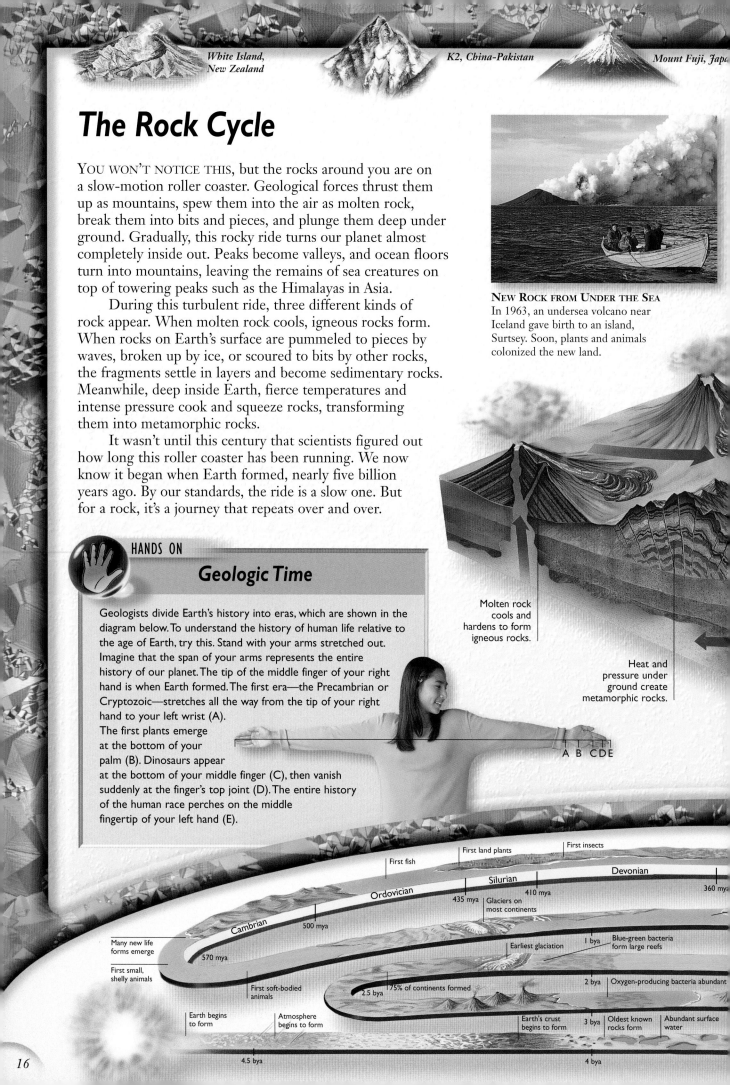

Word Builders

The names of Earth's eras are all made up of the Greek word **zoe**, which means "life," and another Greek word. **Cryptozoic** comes from *crypto*, meaning "hidden." **Paleozoic** includes *paleo*, meaning "ancient." *Meso*, in **Mesozoic**, means "middle." **Cenozoic** comes from *ceno*, meaning "recent."

That's Amazing!

• The oldest known rock lies in Canada's Northwest Territories. The Acasta gneiss, a metamorphic rock, is 3.96 billion years old.
• Lava emerges from Kilauea volcano on Hawaii, U.S.A., at a rate of 7 cubic yards (5 cubic m) per second.

Pathfinder

• Discover what causes plate movements on pages 12–13.
• Find out more about the formation of igneous, sedimentary, and metamorphic rocks on pages 18–23.
• Read about how scientists use fossils to date rock layers on pages 60–61.

ROUND AND ROUND

Everywhere you turn, rocks are on the move. They journey deep into Earth, ̄ly out of exploding volcanoes, and settle ̄ogether at the bottoms of lakes and ̄ceans. As they change their location, ̄ocks also change their appearance.

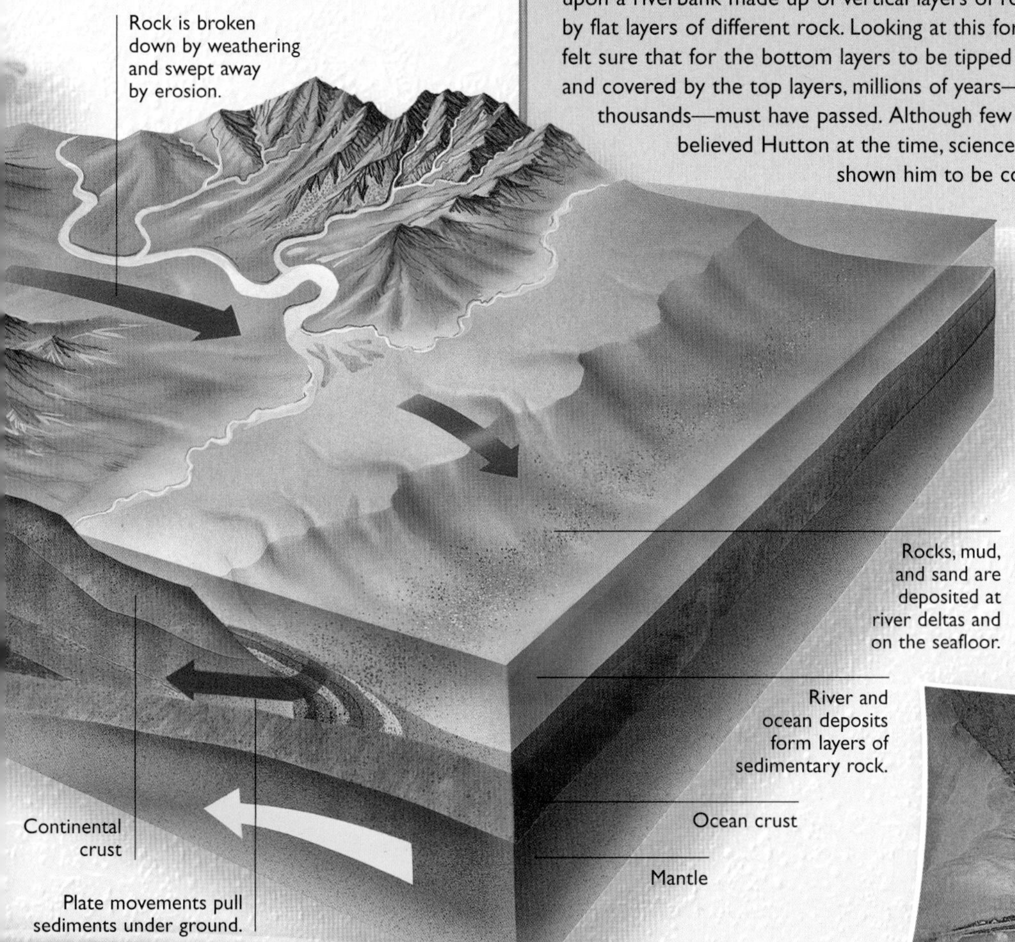

Rock is broken down by weathering and swept away by erosion.

Continental crust

Plate movements pull sediments under ground.

INSIDE STORY

Rock Bottom

Two hundred years ago, people believed that the world was only 6,000 years old. But a Scottish doctor, James Hutton, thought otherwise. Having studied rocks for years, he knew that they changed extremely slowly. One day in 1785, Hutton came upon a riverbank made up of vertical layers of rock topped by flat layers of different rock. Looking at this formation, he felt sure that for the bottom layers to be tipped up on end and covered by the top layers, millions of years—not just thousands—must have passed. Although few people believed Hutton at the time, science has since shown him to be correct.

Rocks, mud, and sand are deposited at river deltas and on the seafloor.

River and ocean deposits form layers of sedimentary rock.

Ocean crust

Mantle

SEDIMENTAL JOURNEY

Where rivers enter the sea, they deposit soil and rocks. These sediments block the river's own path and force it to branch out in different directions. From space, a river mouth (known as a delta) looks like a tree. This picture shows the Mississippi Delta in the U.S.A.

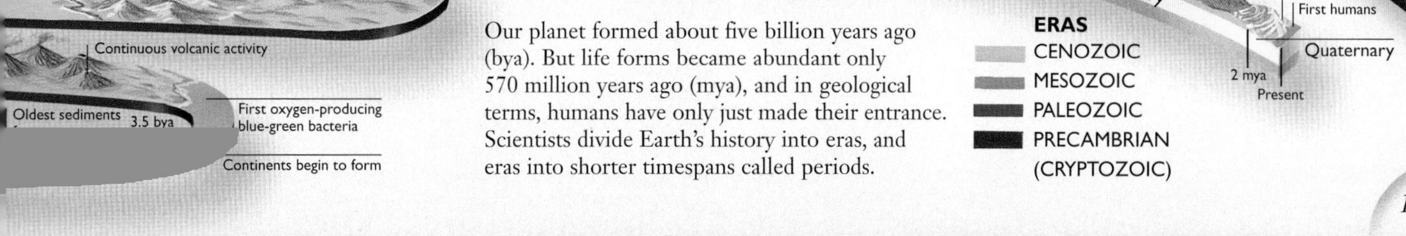

First reptiles

̄phibians

First dinosaurs
First mammals

Carboniferous

Permian

Triassic

Jurassic

First birds

First flowers

First multicellular algae

290 mya

240 mya

205 mya

140 mya

Cretaceous

Extinction of dinosaurs

Himalayas form

Mountain building

1.5 bya

Significant levels of oxygen in atmosphere

EARTH'S AGES

63 mya

Tertiary

Ice Age
First humans

Continuous volcanic activity

Our planet formed about five billion years ago (bya). But life forms became abundant only 570 million years ago (mya), and in geological terms, humans have only just made their entrance. Scientists divide Earth's history into eras, and eras into shorter timespans called periods.

ERAS

CENOZOIC
MESOZOIC
PALEOZOIC
PRECAMBRIAN
(CRYPTOZOIC)

2 mya
Present

Quaternary

Oldest sediments 3.5 bya

First oxygen-producing blue-green bacteria

Continents begin to form

17

Obsidian
(extrusive)

Ropy lava
(extrusive)

Rivers of Fire

RIVERS OF FIRE flow through Earth's crust. They are made of a red-hot mixture of molten rock and crystals called magma, which rises from deep inside the planet. If magma breaks through Earth's surface, it emerges as lava. When magma and lava cool, they harden into a type of rock known as igneous rock. Most of Earth's crust is made of igneous rock, but much of this rock is buried under sediments, seawater, soil, or other rock.

Two kinds of igneous rock occur—intrusive igneous rock and extrusive igneous rock. Intrusive igneous rock forms when magma hardens below the surface. Magma rises through the crust, cramming itself through brittle rock, but it can't always break through. The cooled rock remains under ground until natural forces like erosion and tectonic uplift uncover it. Granite is an intrusive rock that is found when mountain ranges erode down to their cores. Extrusive or volcanic igneous rock forms when magma breaks through the crust as lava and cools on the surface. Basalt is an extrusive rock that makes up ocean crust. Since oceans cover much of Earth, most of Earth's crust is basalt.

Crystals in an igneous rock provide an important clue to how it formed. Intrusive rock cools slowly, producing big crystals you can see easily. Extrusive rock, on the other hand, cools quickly, forming tiny crystals that you can see only with a microscope.

ISLAND BUILDING
Fiery lava frequently flows from Kilauea volcano on the Big Island of Hawaii, U.S.A. As the runny lava cools, it hardens and creates new land. All of the Hawaiian Islands were formed in this way.

Regular, six-sided columns form when lava cools quickly.

INSIDE STORY

The Day the Sky Turned Black

One August afternoon in AD 79, a mountain blew its top. It was Mount Vesuvius, a volcano on the west coast of Italy. The writer Pliny the Younger lived nearby. As ashes rained down, Pliny and his mother fled their house. Above the volcano, "a black and dreadful cloud yawned open to reveal long, fantastic flames," Pliny later wrote. Darkness fell. "You could hear the shrieks of women, the crying of children, and the shouts of men," wrote Pliny. He and his mother had to keep shaking the ashes off themselves, "otherwise we should have been buried and crushed under their weight." But they were among the lucky ones. That day, two towns, Herculaneum and Pompeii, disappeared beneath surges of hot rock, clouds of gas, and mudflows. Centuries later, the towns were uncovered. Lava had hardened around the victims, leaving human-shaped spaces in the rocks after the bodies decayed. Scientists made casts from these molds.

Andesite
(extrusive)

Gabbro
(intrusive)

Word Builders

- **Igneous** comes from the Latin word *ignis*, which means "fire."
- Runny, fast-flowing lava hardens into ropelike coils of rock. In Hawaii, this kind of lava is called **pahoehoe**. Thick, slow-moving lava forms rough, bumpy rock called **aa**. This word is said to come from the sound you would make if you walked barefoot across the rock.

That's Amazing!

In 1815, Mount Tambora in Indonesia exploded in the largest eruption in recorded history. It coughed up 36–43 cubic miles (150–180 cubic km) of hot ash and gas, and killed more than 50,000 people. The ash cloud from the eruption blocked out the Sun for weeks, causing famines that resulted in at least 80,000 additional deaths.

Pathfinder

- Volcanoes occur at the edges of Earth's tectonic plates. Read about tectonic activity on pages 12–13.
- Volcanic plugs are revealed by weathering and erosion. Find out more about these processes on pages 14–15.
- Some igneous rocks contain large crystals. Learn more on pages 28–29.
- How do you identify igneous rocks? Find out on page 54–55.

A ROCK WITH WINGS
Ship Rock in New Mexico, U.S.A., is the remains of an ancient volcano. The local Navajo people call the 1,500-foot (457-m) structure *Tse Bida'hi*, which means "the winged rock."

VOLCANIC PLUGS

Ship Rock is an example of a volcanic plug. These massive stumps of igneous rock have fiery origins. They form when molten rock cools and hardens in the throat of a volcano.

SIX-SIDED STEPS
When lava cools quickly, it can crack and shrink, forming six-sided columns of basalt. These pillars in Northern Ireland are known as the Giant's Causeway. They formed when lava flooded a flat region about 30 million years ago.

Basalt is a dark volcanic rock that is made up of small pyroxene and feldspar crystals.

TOUGH STUFF
Granite is a tough, light-colored rock that usually contains large crystals of feldspar, quartz, and mica.

During eruptions, large amounts of ash and lava pour out of the volcano. The lava-ash mixture cools into igneous rock and forms a cone-shaped mountain.

The eruptions end, and the magma cools and hardens inside the volcano. Weathering and erosion start to wear away the soft exterior of the mountain.

Eventually, natural forces erode the mountain completely. Only the more resistant plug stands as a reminder of the ancient volcano.

19

Conglomerate (rocky sediments)

Sandstone (sandy sediments)

Chert (chemical sediments)

Layer upon Layer

EARTH CHURNS UP rocks, spreads them out, and builds them in layers like a cake. This process starts when weathering and erosion break rocks into tiny pieces. Wind and flowing water then carry the pieces to river, lake, and sea beds, where they settle in layers. As the pieces, or sediments, build up over millions of years, they cement together to form sedimentary rock. Common sedimentary rocks include limestone, sandstone, and shale.

Weathering and erosion cut through soft sedimentary layers like a knife through a cake. But they have to work around tougher sedimentary rock. This creates unusual rock formations as different layers are exposed. Because each layer of rock formed in a separate environment, scientists can study these layers and reconstruct a landscape's history. Some limestone, for example, is made of seashell remains. Sandstone is what's left of a long-gone beach, riverbed, or desert.

Sedimentary rocks also contain useful substances. Coal forms between rock layers when plants from ancient swamps have decayed. Salt, which is sometimes found in layers of sedimentary rock, also forms when seawater evaporates. Did you realize that you were sprinkling your food with the remains of an ocean?

SALT FLATS
Rain and melting snow from distant mountains sometimes transform desert valleys into temporary lakes. When the water evaporates, it leaves behind a layer of salt crystals called a salt flat. This one is in Death Valley, in California, U.S.A.

The lower layers of dark red siltstone and mudstone formed from ancient lowland marshes.

The middle layers of sandstone, siltstone, and mudstone formed under rivers, swamps, and lakes.

HANDS ON
Making Sedimentary Layers

❶ Collect some gravel, coarse sand, fine sand, and a little dirt. Put a few tablespoonfuls of each into a jar and fill the jar halfway with water. With the lid on tight, shake the jar, making sure all the materials mix together.

❷ Leave the mixture to settle overnight. What do you see in the morning? The materials have settled into layers, with the fine sand on top and the heavy gravel at the bottom. This is how sedimentary layers form under water. If you bury the mixture, after a few million years it should turn into sedimentary rock.

CREATING CANYON COUNTRY
Rivers often cut deep into rocks, forming canyons and gorges. As the canyon walls wear away, the valleys get bigger, and flat-topped mountains form.

Sedimentary rocks are exposed when the sea level falls or the land is uplifted. Rivers cut deep into rocks, forming narrow pathways in the land.

Word Builders
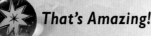

• The word **sedimentary** comes from the Latin *sedimentum*, which means "settling," and also from the Latin verb *sedere*, which means "to sink" or "to sit down."
• **Canyons** are steep-sided valleys. Canyon comes from the Spanish word *caña,* meaning "tube."

That's Amazing!

The sedimentary rocks dolomite and limestone usually contain pieces of shells that once belonged to tiny marine creatures called foraminifera. These single-celled animals are so small that one whole shell can fit inside the eye of a needle.

Pathfinder

• Discover more about weathering and erosion on pages 14–15.
• Sedimentary rocks often contain fossils. These are used by geologists to date rock layers. Go to pages 46–47.
• Learn how coal forms and take a look inside a coal mine on pages 48–49.

FROM THE DEEP
This odd-looking rock is a shelly limestone. It began to form when sea creatures died and their shells sank to the seafloor. Over time, the shells were cemented into a solid lump.

THE STUFF OF ANCIENT WATERS

Capitol Reef, in Utah, U.S.A., was named by a group of early settlers because the cliffs blocked their way just as a reef would at sea. Most of these sedimentary rocks formed about 200 million years ago under rivers and swamps.

INSIDE STORY

Clinging to a Canyon

One-armed geologist and soldier General John Wesley Powell clings to a canyon wall high above the Colorado River. It is 1869, and he and his men are conducting the first survey of the river's sedimentary canyons. He climbed up here with his friend G. Y. Bradley to look for a safe route over the rapids. But now, with his foot wedged into a crack and his left hand grasping a rocky overhang, Powell is stuck. He calls for help. Bradley finds a way to the top of the rock but cannot reach the general. Suddenly he gets an idea. He takes off his pants and swings them down. Powell grasps them tightly, and Bradley hauls him up. Without Bradley's quick thinking, Powell's geological knowledge may have been lost forever.

The hard red sandstone cap resists erosion. It formed from ancient desert sand dunes.

This greenish gray shale contains volcanic ash.

THE WHITE CLIFFS OF DOVER
These cliffs at Dover in England are a type of powdery limestone called chalk. A thumb-sized chunk of this rock contains thousands of microscopic shell pieces that are about 70 million years old.

As the rivers cut deeper into the hard, resistant rock, they form steep-sided valleys. When they reach softer layers, the rivers start to dig under the hard rock.

The undercutting causes the upper layers to collapse, and the valley widens. This creates large, flat-topped rocks called mesas and small ones called buttes.

Quartzite

Folded schist

Banded gneiss

Squeezed and Baked

DEEP INSIDE Earth's crust, pressure-cooker conditions transform rocks into new types. These altered rocks are called metamorphic rocks. Some develop when they are squeezed and folded under the massive weight of mountains. Others form when the blistering heat of magma bakes them into something new. All kinds of rock—igneous rocks, sedimentary rocks, and even other metamorphic rocks—can change under these extreme conditions.

You might think that such harsh environments would destroy rock. But they actually make it stronger. Think of how snow becomes harder when you squeeze it into a more compact ball. The same thing happens to rocks. When limestone, a rock with tiny pores, is squeezed, it changes into marble, a stone with larger, better-cemented grains. Flaky shale becomes the more durable slate, the material used in the chalkboard your teacher writes on.

We catch a glimpse of the world beneath Earth's crust when metamorphic rocks become exposed. This happens when wind, water, and other natural forces attack the land covering the rocks. As weaker rocks wear away, the tough metamorphic rocks hold firm, emerging from Earth's crust to form mountain ranges of baked and twisted stone.

A STONE OF MANY COLORS
Marble forms in a wide range of colors, depending on the minerals present in the rock.

SPLIT MOUNTAIN
At Split Mountain in California, U.S.A, a dark layer of metamorphic rock sits on top of a lighter layer of igneous rock. The igneous rock was once a large bubble, or intrusion, of magma. The magma heated the sedimentary rock above it, turning it into metamorphic rock.

This massive block of granite, an igneous rock, formed when magma cooled.

The metamorphic rock formed when sedimentary rock was baked by magma.

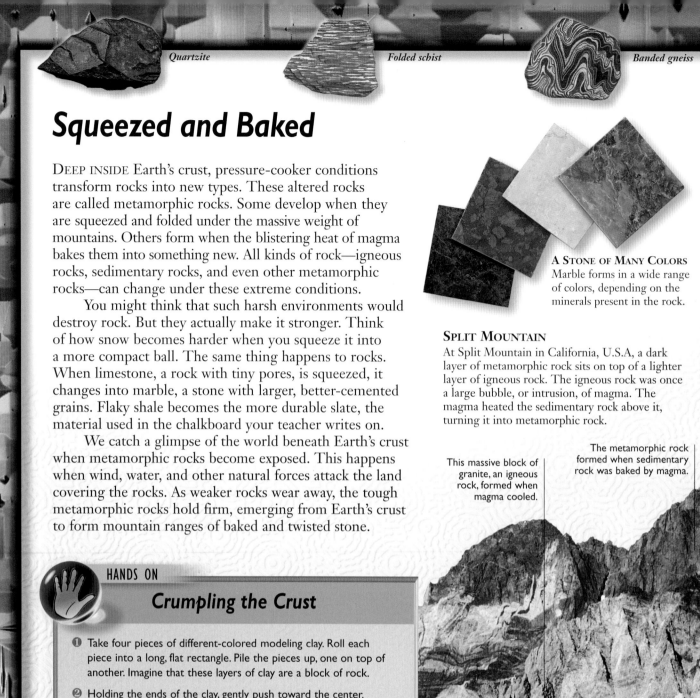

HANDS ON

Crumpling the Crust

❶ Take four pieces of different-colored modeling clay. Roll each piece into a long, flat rectangle. Pile the pieces up, one on top of another. Imagine that these layers of clay are a block of rock.

❷ Holding the ends of the clay, gently push toward the center. As you do, the clay will buckle and form folds. A similar thing occurs inside Earth's crust when tectonic plates collide. The crust folds, forming mountains. If they are squeezed hard enough, the rocks beneath the mountains change into other rocks. This process is called regional metamorphism.

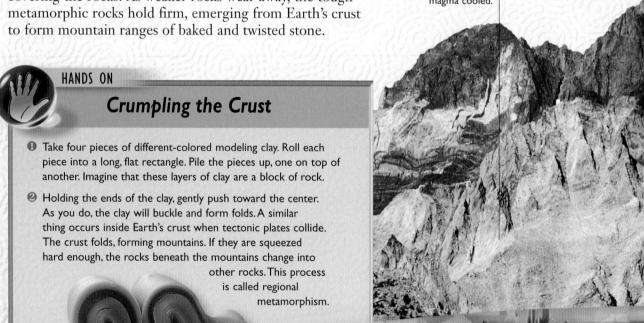

REGIONAL METAMORPHISM

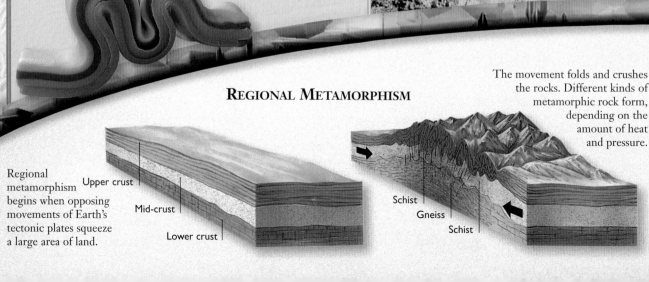

Regional metamorphism begins when opposing movements of Earth's tectonic plates squeeze a large area of land.

Upper crust

Mid-crust

Lower crust

The movement folds and crushes the rocks. Different kinds of metamorphic rock form, depending on the amount of heat and pressure.

Schist

Gneiss

Schist

Word Builders

• **Metamorphic** and **metamorphism** are both made up of the Greek words *meta*, meaning "change," and *morphe*, meaning "form."
• **Gneiss** (pronounced "nice") comes from an Old Norse word *gneista,* meaning "to give off sparks."

That's Amazing!

Metamorphism can turn a rock into one of a number of other rocks, depending on the amount of heat and pressure involved. For example, shale can turn into slate (moderate heat and pressure), schist (high heat and pressure), or gneiss (extreme heat and pressure).

Pathfinder

• Find out how colliding tectonic plates cause Earth's crust to crumple on pages 12–13.
• Metamorphic rocks may contain gemstones. Turn to pages 34–35.
• Learn how to identify metamorphic rocks on pages 54–55.

METAMORPHIC MONUMENT
Emperor Shah Jahan built this tomb, known as the Taj Mahal, at Agra in India, as a monument to his wife, Mumtaz. It was constructed between 1632 and 1654 and is made entirely of white marble.

INSIDE STORY

Seeing Is Believing

Geologist Sir James Hall picked up his gun. He was determined to prove a point. His good friend, James Hutton, believed that heat and pressure could change chalky rocks like limestone and dolomite into marble. Other scientists laughed at this, but Sir James agreed with his friend. To prove it, he poured powdered chalk down the gun barrel, sealed the end, and roasted the weapon. Once it cooled, he tipped out a stony mass that looked like marble. Hutton was right! Not everyone was convinced. But Sir James went on to conduct 500 similar experiments between 1798 and 1805. Today, everyone agrees with him and Hutton.

UNDER PRESSURE
The rock in this cliff face used to be shale. Extreme pressure turned it into a new type of rock called slate.

CONTACT METAMORPHISM

Sandstone
Shale
Limestone
Magma

Quartzite
Hornfels
Marble
Magma

Contact metamorphism occurs when magma rises through rock. The magma chamber may be as big as a mountain or as small as a house.

The magma bakes the surrounding stone. Depending on the kind of rock present, different types of metamorphic rock form.

23

Dumbbell micrometeorite

Pyrite sand dollar

Pumice

Strange Rocks

JUST WHEN YOU THINK you have rocks figured out, a few odd ones pop up. Take meteoroids, for example. They rocket in from outer space, grazing the night sky in a streak of light. You might know them as shooting stars. But they aren't stars. They are chunks of black, heavy rock. When they zip through the atmosphere, friction causes them to burn brightly. In the past, enormous meteoroids have slammed into Earth, creating huge craters. Then the rocks are called meteorites. Fortunately for us, most of these flying rocks burn up in Earth's atmosphere.

Not all peculiar rocks come from space. For example, there is a type of sandstone called itacolumite that you can bend and twist with your bare hands, as easily as you can bend a piece of wire. This is possible because itacolumite contains flexible minerals linked together inside the rock. There is also a common type of volcanic rock that is so light that it floats in water. It is called pumice.

Other rocks just look strange. Pseudofossils are rocks that resemble fossils. People have often mistaken them for traces of prehistoric plants or animals. Some rocks look like live plants. You'd think a desert rose ought to be in a vase. But it's really a rock made of a mineral called gypsum.

RACING ROCKS
In Death Valley, in California, U.S.A., chunks of rock lie next to trails, as if they have been racing across the mud. Scientists believe that the rocks are lifted by sheets of ice that form on the lake when it fills in winter. As the ice drifts across the water, it trails the rocks along the lake bed.

CRYSTAL BALLS
Geodes are balls of rock that contain crystals. On the outside, they look plain and dull. But if you crack one open, you may get a surprise.

FLOWERS OF THE DESERT
Some "flowers" are made of rock. These gypsum roses form in deserts when groundwater containing calcium and sulfur evaporates. The gypsum that is left behind forms crystals. The crystals grow over the grains of sand, binding them into a roselike pattern.

BUBBLING UNDER
Geodes form in cavities inside igneous or sedimentary rocks. They emerge when the rock is worn away by erosion or weathering.

When igneous or sedimentary rock layers form, cavities may be created by gas bubbles. Water containing dissolved minerals sometimes seeps into the cavities.

Word Builders

As rocks hurtle through space, they are called **meteoroids**. If they fall to Earth, friction in the atmosphere causes them to make streaks of light, which we call **meteors**. Any rock that doesn't get burned up and makes it to Earth's surface gets the name **meteorite**.

That's Amazing!

• Up to 100,000 tons of rock fall into Earth's atmosphere each year.
• The largest meteorite in the world lies in the ground on the Hoba farm near Grootfontein in Namibia, Africa. It weighs 60 tons (59 tonnes) and measures 9 feet (2.7 m) long, 8 feet (2.4 m) wide, and 3 feet (0.9 m) thick.

Pathfinder

• It's not just rocks that can be strange. Find out about the unusual properties of minerals on pages 38–39.
• Take a trip to the Moon with the first geologist in space on page 46.
• Crystals form inside all rocks, not just geodes. Learn how to identify crystals in rocks on pages 54–55.

NATURAL SCULPTURES
Pseudofossils are oddly shaped rocks that look like the remains of ancient life forms. They may resemble plants, animals, or even humans.

INSIDE STORY

Strike It Rich

On October 9, 1992, Michelle Knapp sat at home in Peekskill, New York, U.S.A. Suddenly, she heard a loud bang. "It sounded like a three-car crash," she said later. She ran outside to investigate. The rear of her car looked like someone had punched a huge hole in it. Peeking under the trunk, she found a rock the size of a small watermelon, smelling like rotten eggs. It was a meteorite. The meteorite wasn't all bad news, however. Collectors paid Michelle's family $69,000 for the rock. They even bought the car, which was worth $300, for $10,000.

ROCKS FROM OUTER SPACE
Meteorites, like this one found in the Atacama Desert in Chile, are true space aliens. Most are chunks of rock that broke off asteroids or planets. By studying these extraterrestrials, scientists can learn about the history of the solar system.

IN A FLASH
Wiry stones called fulgurites form when lightning zaps soil, sand, or rock. The lightning heats a strip of the material, which melts and cools into a long, pipelike shape.

The mineral-rich water deposits concentric layers of tiny crystals on the walls of the rock cavity. Each layer may be a different color.

If there is not enough water to fill the cavity completely, a space may remain at the center. Sometimes, quartz crystals grow inside this space.

Minerals

LOOK CLOSELY AT a rock and you may notice that it is made up of tiny pieces of one or more materials. These materials are called minerals. Minerals are the building blocks of rocks. They are solid chemical substances that form within Earth (as well as on other planets). There are thousands of different minerals, and they come in all colors, shapes, and sizes. They include metals such as gold and silver, as well as valuable gemstones such as diamonds. Minerals may form regular, flat-sided shapes called crystals. Often, crystals of different minerals grow together, forming rocks. When minerals have plenty of space to grow, they form large, beautiful crystals.

Copper: dendritic (treelike) habit

Labradorite: massive (rocklike) habit

Garnet: equant (equal-sided) habit

Meet the Minerals

MINERALS ARE solid substances that occur naturally in Earth's crust. They are made up of chemicals called elements. Eight elements make up 99 percent of all minerals on Earth. They are oxygen, silicon, aluminum, iron, magnesium, calcium, potassium, and sodium. A mineral that contains only one element is called a native element. If more than one element makes up a mineral, it is called a compound.

Just like you, minerals contain tiny particles called atoms. If you could shrink yourself down to microscopic size, you would see that the atoms in most minerals form a repeating, three-dimensional pattern. This makes a mineral grow into a crystal with a regular shape and flat sides. Some crystals form cubes. Others grow into columns with three or more sides, which are called prisms. Often, minerals grow together with other minerals in irregular masses known as rocks. In these cases, the crystals may be so small that you cannot see them. But they still possess a regular internal structure.

Scientists have identified more than 2,500 different minerals. We can recognize minerals by examining their color, density, hardness, and habit. The habit of a mineral is the overall shape formed by its crystals. It depends on the internal structure of the crystals and the conditions in which they grow. Some habits are very unusual. There are minerals that look like piles of needles, bunches of grapes, and even tiny trees.

CRYSTAL STRANDS
Bundles of crystal strands make up this piece of amphibole asbestos, giving it a fibrous habit. Asbestos fibers won't burn, so asbestos was often used as fireproofing material before some varieties were proven to be a health hazard.

ROCK CANDY
Wulfenite usually forms flat tablet-like crystals. This is called a tabular habit. The shape of the crystals and their butterscotch color make them look like candy. Wulfenite crystals are often transparent. They sometimes contain wispy patterns, known as phantoms, that form when traces of other minerals are trapped in the crystals.

A VARIED WARDROBE
Many minerals come in a variety of colors. For example, fluorite shows up in several shades, including green, yellow, and purple. The colors are caused by impurities in the mineral.

Word Builders

• The word **mineral** comes from the Latin word *minera*, which means "mine" or "ore."
• **Crystal** comes from the Greek word *crystallos*, meaning "ice." The ancient Greeks believed that quartz was made of water that had frozen so hard it would never melt.
• **Rhodochrosite** gets its name from the Greek words *rhodon*, meaning "rose," and *chros*, meaning "color."

That's Amazing!

• The largest topaz crystal in the world was found in Brazil in 1940. It weighs 596 pounds (270 kg) and is on display in the American Museum of Natural History, New York, U.S.A.
• In South Dakota, U.S.A., miners found crystals of a mineral called spodumene that measure 47 feet (14.3 m) in length and weigh 80 tons (72.8 metric tons).

Pathfinder

• Find out how to identify rocks and minerals on pages 54–55.
• Azurite contains copper. Learn more about this metal on pages 30–31.
• Large crystals are common in igneous and metamorphic rocks. See pages 18–19, 22–23.
• Some people believe that minerals have magical powers. Turn to pages 38–39.

MAMMOTH MINERALS

Tiny crystals can grow into mammoth minerals. Crystals grow at different rates, but each one retains its internal structure. The topaz crystal below has a columnar shape called a prismatic habit. It developed this form while maturing into a 111-pound (50.3-kg) giant. People cut such crystals into huge gemstones. The cut gem shown below left is called the American Golden Topaz. It weighs 10 pounds (4.5 kg).

HANDS ON
Grow Your Own Crystals

You can grow your own crystals at home using salt and water.

❶ Stir salt into a jar of warm water until no more will dissolve. Attach a thread to a pencil and hang it above the solution.

❷ As the water evaporates, cubic salt crystals will form on the thread. Salt forms cubic crystals because its molecules are arranged in a cubic pattern that repeats itself as the salt grows.

❸ To encourage large crystals, break off the smallest crystals and throw them away. If your crystals stop growing, add more salt.

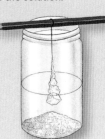

TRUE BLUE
Azurite shows up in different habits, but always in a deep blue color. Sometimes it grows in this botryoidal habit, making the mineral look like a bunch of grapes. People often polish azurite and use it to make jewelry.

NATURAL NEEDLES
Crocoite often grows with an acicular, or needlelike, habit. This rare and fragile mineral is a favorite with collectors. Some of the best specimens come from mines on the island of Tasmania in Australia.

THE SAME OLD CLOTHES
A number of minerals sport one color all of the time. For example, rhodochrosite is always a rosy pink. Malachite is usually rich green. And sulfur comes in nothing but bright yellow.

Bornite
(copper ore)

Galena
(lead ore)

Bauxite
(aluminum ore)

Earth's Riches

EARTH BOASTS a treasure trove of useful minerals. These include metals such as gold, silver, copper, and lead, and nonmetallic minerals such as sulfur and salt. Minerals that are useful to people and can be mined economically are called ores. These minerals have been valued and collected by humans for thousands of years.

One of the first ores to be mined was copper. It may form in the ground as a lump of pure metal, making it easy to recognize and collect. Other metals, such as gold, silver, and platinum also occur in this pure state. We call these minerals native metals. However, most metals mix with other elements to form minerals in rocks. Aluminum, for example, is combined with oxygen in a rock called bauxite. Lead, which rarely appears in a pure state, is found in minerals such as galena and cerussite. It took humans thousands of years to learn how to separate metals from rocks.

Metals are not the only useful materials obtained from rocks. People also gather a range of nonmetallic minerals. For example, we use graphite to make pencils. We heat gypsum to make plaster of paris. We even mine rocks to add to our food. Did you realize that you regularly eat a mineral called halite? It's more commonly known as salt.

LIQUID ROCK
These silvery beads are drops of mercury, the only metal that exists as a liquid at room temperature. It forms in cinnabar, a reddish ore. We use this metal in thermometers because it is sensitive to small changes in temperature and gives us accurate readings.

BEAUTIFUL BRIMSTONE
Sulfur is a bright yellow nonmetallic mineral. It forms near hot springs and volcanic vents. In ancient times, it was known as "brimstone" or "the fuel of Hell's fires." Sulfur looks beautiful, but it easily combines with hydrogen to form hydrogen sulfide, which stinks like rotten eggs. Despite this, people use sulfur to make fertilizers and chemicals that kill insects.

MAKING STEEL

Steel is a mixture of iron and carbon. We use it to make a wide range of objects, from cars and utensils to trains and tools. Producing steel involves many complicated processes. These illustrations show the main steps.

Iron ore

Coke

Limestone

Steel is made from iron, coke (a type of heated coal), and limestone. The iron must first be extracted from iron ore, which usually contains iron and oxygen.

Slag
Iron

The ingredients are put into a furnace that may stand 25 stories high. Workers then blast hot air into the furnace to raise the temperature. The coke combines with the oxygen in the ore to form carbon monoxide. The molten iron sinks to the bottom of the furnace. Adding limestone removes impurities, forming a waste material called slag.

Word Builders

• The word **copper** comes from the Greek name for the island of Cyprus, *Kyprios,* where copper was first mined five thousand years ago.
• **Hematite** is a major iron ore. When ground up, it forms a red powder. Its name comes from the Greek word *haimatites,* which means "bloodlike."
• **Bauxite** is named for the town of Les Baux in France, where this ore was first discovered in 1821.

That's Amazing!

• It takes four tons of bauxite to produce one ton of aluminum.
• A bucket filled with a gallon of water weighs 8.5 pounds (3.8 kg). The same bucket filled with liquid mercury would weigh 115 pounds (52 kg). Mercury is so dense that a piece of lead will float on its surface like a boat on the sea.

Pathfinder

• Which are the most valuable metals? Find out on pages 32–33.
• Most modern buildings are reinforced with steel. See pages 8–9 and 42–43.
• Strong, lightweight metals such as aluminum and titanium are used to build planes, helicopters, and even spacecraft. Turn to pages 50–51.

THE COLORS OF COPPER

Copper occurs both as a native metal and in a number of ores. The native form (below left) is reddish, and often looks like a clump of wires. But when copper combines with other elements, the resulting minerals are usually blue or green. Copper ores include this turquoise-colored rock called aurichalcite (far left) and this deep blue mineral, azurite (right).

SLENDER SPIKES OF STIBNITE
They may look like pins in a pincushion, but these are actually crystals of stibnite. Stibnite is the principal ore of a metal called antimony.

INSIDE STORY

Coppersmiths of Ancient Israel

My name is Solomon. I live in the valley of Timna in Israel. My people are coppersmiths. We mine copper for the Egyptian pharaoh. The copper we mine comes from a green mineral called malachite. I help my father and brother to separate the copper from the malachite, using a process called smelting. We fill a stone furnace with charcoal and then blow air through pipes to make the coals hotter. My brother and I keep blowing while my father sprinkles crushed malachite into the furnace and adds more charcoal. After a while, we let the furnace cool. Black lumps of waste called slag form at the bottom. We smash open the slag and retrieve pellets of copper. It's hard work, but our copper has made us famous throughout Egypt.

The iron is poured into another furnace that contains steel scraps. Heated oxygen is blasted into the iron to keep it hot and to combine with excess carbon. This reduces the amount of carbon in the iron, turning it into steel.

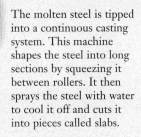

The molten steel is tipped into a continuous casting system. This machine shapes the steel into long sections by squeezing it between rollers. It then sprays the steel with water to cool it off and cuts it into pieces called slabs.

Sheet-metal workers bend, cut, and roll the slabs into a range of shapes, including wires, girders, sheets, and pipes. These items are then sold to manufacturers who use them to make a wide variety of products.

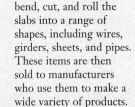

Wire

Girders

Sheets

Pipes

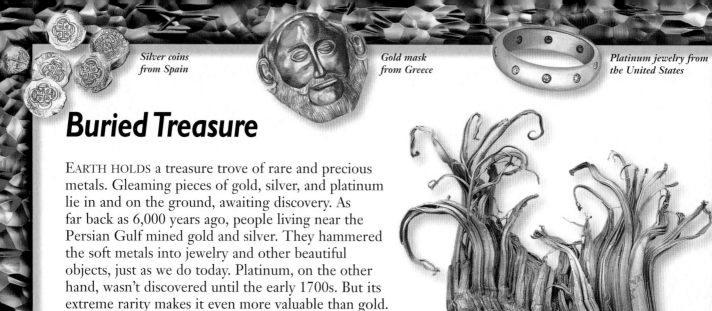

Silver coins from Spain

Gold mask from Greece

Platinum jewelry from the United States

Buried Treasure

EARTH HOLDS a treasure trove of rare and precious metals. Gleaming pieces of gold, silver, and platinum lie in and on the ground, awaiting discovery. As far back as 6,000 years ago, people living near the Persian Gulf mined gold and silver. They hammered the soft metals into jewelry and other beautiful objects, just as we do today. Platinum, on the other hand, wasn't discovered until the early 1700s. But its extreme rarity makes it even more valuable than gold.

Precious metals often occur in their pure, or native, state. They turn up in veins—mineral deposits that fill cracks in Earth's crust. We also find them mixed with sand and gravel on riverbeds. These deposits, called placer ores, form when erosion separates the metal from rock and water washes it into a river, where it sinks to the bottom. This often happens to gold.

Gold frequently finds its way into beautiful jewelry. But it has properties that make it valuable in industry, too. For example, gold does not rust, so it is often used to make vital pieces of electronic equipment. The metal is also very shiny. When used as a coating on the outside of satellites and other space instruments, gold reflects cosmic radiation that would otherwise damage the equipment.

SILVER STRINGS
Treelike strands of native silver form where hot liquids deposit minerals. A small amount of mined silver is made into coins, jewelry, and utensils. But the most common use of this metal is in photographic film. When you take a photo, silver crystals are produced from the film emulsion. The crystals react to the light and capture the image.

INSIDE STORY

The Gold Rush

My name is Pete. I'm a prospector panning for gold in the hills of northern California. I used to live in Boston, in the eastern United States, where I worked as a banker. Then I read in the newspaper that a man had found gold here in the American River. So I quit my job and headed west to San Francisco. On the way out here, I passed abandoned farms and businesses—everyone is joining the gold rush. I arrived in the beginning of 1849, so folks call me a forty-niner. Soon, I hope they'll call me rich.

PRIZE PLATINUM
Platinum nuggets are seldom larger than a pea. This one, shown at actual size, would qualify as a major find. The highest quality platinum comes from the Ural Mountains in Russia. We use platinum for jewelry, but it also plays less glamorous roles. For example, it is placed in antipollution devices in cars to trap dirt and toxic gases.

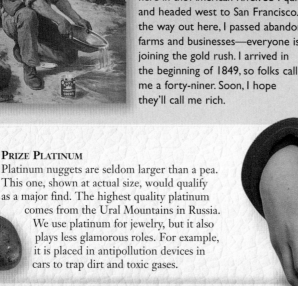

• **Platinum** comes from the Spanish word *plata,* meaning "silver." The name refers to the color of the metal.
• For centuries, people used **pyrite** to make fire. If you strike the mineral against flint or iron, it produces sparks. The word "pyrite" comes from the Greek word *pyr,* meaning "fire."
• The chemical symbol for silver is **Ag**, which comes from its Latin name *argentum,* meaning "white and shining."

• The biggest pure-gold nugget ever found was discovered at Moliagul, in Victoria, Australia, in 1869. Named the Welcome Stranger, it weighed in at 156 pounds (70.8 kg).
• Platinum is so rare that 2 million pounds (907,000 kg) of ore may contain only one pound (0.45 kg) of metal.
• Gold is so soft and easily worked that you could roll an ounce (28 g) of it into a hair-thin wire 50 miles (80 km) long.

• Gold, silver, and platinum are all native elements. Find out more about native elements on pages 28–29.
• Precious metals are sometimes extracted from ores. Go to pages 30–31.
• Take a look at some beautiful gold objects on pages 44–45.
• To learn about tests used to identify minerals, go to page 55.

DON'T BE FOOLED
Prospectors often mistook this shiny, yellow mineral called pyrite for gold. This earned it the name "fool's gold." But you don't have to be tricked. You can tell the difference between gold and pyrite by scratching the minerals across a piece of unglazed white porcelain. Pyrite leaves a greenish-black mark, while gold streaks yellow.

GOLD NUGGETS
Gold nuggets as large as these ones are rare finds. These are plaster casts of a pair of nuggets found at Rheola, in Victoria, Australia, in 1870. They are called the Viscount and Viscountess of Canterbury. If the nuggets were real, these children wouldn't be able to pick them up—gold is twice as heavy as lead.

GOLD GROWTH
Some gold nuggets may grow in sediments like potatoes grow in soil. Scientists now think that these nuggets form when miniscule flecks of gold carried by water attach themselves to bacteria.

Microscopic strands of bacteria in sediments attract tiny, dissolved molecules of gold present in wet ground. Static electricity makes the gold stick to the bacteria, just as pieces of paper will stick to a rubber ballon that you have rubbed on your hair.

More gold builds up and solidifies on the bacteria, coating it like a suit of armor. Gradually, the gold thickens, filling the gaps between the strands while the bacteria continue to grow outward.

Over time, a microscopic nugget forms. The lump continues to attract tiny pieces of dissolved gold. Eventually, it may grow as large as the nuggets on the left.

This photograph was taken through a microscope. It shows a thin layer of gold coating a tangled mass of bacteria. The top has been worn smooth by erosion.

Rare Beauty

SOME MINERALS are in a class of their own. Known as gemstones, they are collected and treasured for their outstanding beauty. The most valuable gemstones, called precious gems, have two additional qualities. They are rare and durable. People seek rare stones because they like to own unique objects. They value hard gems because these minerals retain their beauty without scratching or breaking for a long time. Precious gems include diamonds, rubies, sapphires, and emeralds.

Some gemstones form during metamorphism—when rocks in the crust are buried, squeezed, and heated by plate movements. For example, rubies may form when sedimentary rock is transformed by mountain formation. On the other hand, diamonds grow deep under ground in Earth's upper mantle, and emeralds form when liquids crystallize in or around cooling granite. The hardness of a gemstone depends on the size, arrangement, and types of its atoms.

Gemstones may be carried to the surface by eruptions or plate movements and then exposed by erosion. Running water may dislodge gems from rock layers and leave them on riverbeds. These deposits are called placer deposits. Uncovering precious stones can be like hunting for a needle in a haystack. Miners often have to dig up 500 tons (454 tonnes) of ore to locate a single ounce (28 g) of diamond.

KING OF THE GEMS

Diamond is the hardest natural substance on Earth. It also possesses a fiery brilliance unmatched by any other gemstone. Many diamonds appear colorless, or clear, but most have a slight tinge of yellow. The famous 128-carat Tiffany Diamond, seen here, sparkles canary yellow. Other "fancy" colors include pink, green, blue, purple, and red—the rarest of all.

RUBY RED

Ruby (left) and sapphire are two types of a mineral called corundum. If a tiny amount of chromium mixes with corundum, the mineral is red and is called ruby. The red color of ruby varies from pale red to purple. Blood-red ruby is among the rarest and most valuable of gems. Rubies are also used to make certain lasers.

UNDER PRESSURE

Diamonds form about 90 miles (145 km) or more below the ground, in the upper mantle. The gems are carried to the surface during the formation of an igneous rock called kimberlite. Here are the basics of kimberlite formation.

Extreme pressure in the upper mantle compresses carbon molecules into diamond crystals. The kimberlite magma that contains the diamonds rises toward the surface, buoyed up by the denser surrounding mantle. Gas bubbles form in the magma as it moves up into the crust.

Word Builders

- **Tourmaline** derives from the Sinhalese (Sri Lankan) word *touramalli*, meaning "stones of mixed colors."
- **Diamond** comes from the Greek word *adamas*, meaning "invincible."
- **Ruby** takes its name from the Latin word *rubeus*, meaning "red."
- **Corundum** comes from the Sanskrit word *kuruvinda*, meaning "ruby."

That's Amazing!

- The largest diamond ever found was the 3,106-carat Cullinan. Discovered in South Africa in 1905, it was cut into 9 large jewels and 96 smaller ones.
- Corundum is the second-hardest mineral after diamond. However, diamond is approximately 150 times harder than corundum.

Pathfinder

- More common gemstones are known as semiprecious stones. Find out about these minerals on pages 36–37.
- For centuries, people believed that gems had magical powers. Read about magical minerals on pages 38–39.
- A gem called topaz may form enormous crystals. Take a look at a giant topaz on pages 28–29.

INSIDE STORY

The Punch Diamond

In April 1928, 12-year-old William Jones—nicknamed Punch—made a remarkable discovery. Punch and his father, Grover, were pitching horseshoes in their backyard at Petertown, West Virginia, U.S.A. As one of the horseshoes landed, the father and son heard a loud "clang." When Punch brushed away the dirt, he saw a bluish-white crystal the size of a large marble gleaming in the sunlight. "See, I have found a diamond," he said to his father. They both laughed at this idea. Punch put the crystal into a cigar box, and it remained there for 15 years. In 1943, Grover took the stone to an expert. He confirmed that it was actually a 34.48 carat diamond—one of the largest ever found in the eastern United States. The Jones family put the Punch Diamond, as it was now known, on display in a museum. Then, in 1984, they sold it. The bluish stone, found in a dusty horseshoe pit, fetched $74,250.

SEARCHING FOR SAPPHIRES
This collector is searching for sapphires by using a pump to suck up river sediments. He will then pass the sediments through a sieve. As he swirls the sediments around on the sieve, centrifugal force pushes the lighter stones such as quartz to the outside, leaving the heavier red zircons and blue sapphires in the center (above right).

RAW DIAMOND

Diamonds like the one on the left are commonly found in a rock called kimberlite. They usually form eight-sided crystals called octahedrons, which look like two pyramids glued together at the base.

WATERMELON TOURMALINE
With its green "rind" and pink "flesh," this tourmaline crystal looks like a chunk of watermelon. Tourmaline displays a great variety of colors. It can be pink, red, blue, green, violet, yellow, orange, brown, black, or even crystal clear. The color depends on the metals present in the mineral. Pink is caused by manganese, while green may be due to iron or chromium.

Every so often, a buildup of gas or a physical reaction between the magma and groundwater results in an explosive volcanic eruption. This blasts molten rock, rocky material, and diamonds up through the crust. The last event of this kind probably occurred about 60 million years ago.

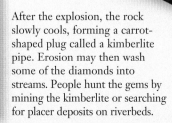

After the explosion, the rock slowly cools, forming a carrot-shaped plug called a kimberlite pipe. Erosion may then wash some of the diamonds into streams. People hunt the gems by mining the kimberlite or searching for placer deposits on riverbeds.

When they were found, these stones looked rough and colorless. But polishing the stones completely transforms them, and we can now see their glorious colors.

Clockwise from top left: amazonite, jasper, tiger's eye, rhodonite, snowflake obsidian, hematite, lace agate, bloodstone

Nephrite

Colors and Shapes

SOME GEMSTONES are plentiful as well as beautiful. Because they are more common, these stones are less valuable than rare, precious gems. But we still collect and treasure them, usually for their rich colors or patterns. People sometimes refer to these gems as ornamental or semiprecious stones. For thousands of years, humans have used ornamental stones to enhance clothes, jewelry, and art. For example, people in France made jewelry out of polished pieces of a reddish stone called jasper as long as 20,000 years ago.

Ornamentals often occur as clumps of tiny, intergrown crystals. This is known as a massive habit, since no regular crystal shapes can be seen. Certain combinations of crystals create amazing patterns. Agate, for instance, contains wavy bands of color. They are formed by alternating layers of small chalcedony crystals containing slightly different chemicals and may occur with larger quartz crystals.

Other types of gemstones, called organic gems, are created by plants and animals. For example, pearls grow inside shellfish. The skeletons of sea creatures create coral. And jet, a black gemstone, is a variety of coal, a rock formed from animal or plant remains.

TWO IN ONE
Jade is the name given to either of two different minerals: nephrite and jadeite. Both are tough and come in a variety of colors. The people of New Zealand have been carving nephrite into artworks and tools like these knives since AD 1000.

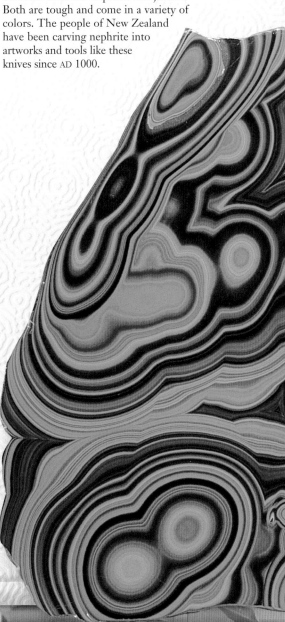

ULTRA BLUE
Lapis lazuli is treasured for its rich blue color and is often used in jewelry. The ancient Egyptians also used powdered lapis lazuli as eye shadow. In Renaissance Europe, artists used the same powder to make a highly prized paint called ultramarine. In this painting, "St. Francis Giving His Cloak to a Poor Soldier" (1437), the artist Sassetta used ultramarine to emphasize the value of the cloak.

Lapis lazuli

GEMS THAT GROW
A pearl begins to form when a piece of grit or a grain of sand lodges inside the shell of an oyster, clam, or mussel.

To protect itself from this irritant, the animal inside covers the grit with a substance called nacre. The nacre builds up in layers and, in seven years or so, forms a pearl.

Word Builders

- Merchants from Venice used to purchase **turquoise** in Turkish markets and then sell it to Europeans. As a result, the French people who bought the gemstone referred to it as *pierre turquoise,* or "Turkish stone."
- **Lapis lazuli** comes from the Latin word for "stone," *lapis,* and the Arabic *lazaward,* meaning "heaven" or "sky."

That's Amazing!

- The Pueblo people of North America used to place turquoise beads in their tombs. One burial site known as Pueblo Bonito, in New Mexico, U.S.A., contains about 24,900 of these beads.
- The highest-quality lapis lazuli comes from the mountains of Badakhshan in Afghanistan. People have been mining this source for more than 6,000 years.

Pathfinder

- Most ornamental stones form in massive habits. Find out about mineral habits on pages 28–29.
- Colorful stones called agates often line geode cavities. See pages 24–25.
- Ornamental stones have been used in jewelry for centuries. See pages 44–45.
- Amber is an organic gem. It looks like a mineral but is actually fossilized tree sap. Sometimes it contains ancient life forms. Take a look at one on page 60.

HANDS ON

Rock and Roll

In their natural state, most ornamental stones are rough and dull. To bring out their colors and patterns, collectors polish the stones using a tumbling machine. This consists of a hollow drum that is rotated by motor-driven rollers. You can buy tumbling machines, but the best way to learn how to use one is to join a lapidary club. These groups collect and polish ornamental stones, and use them to make jewelry.

To tumble stones, you place the rocks into the drum with water and coarse grit. Then you turn on the machine and leave it running for a week or so. Next, you replace the grit with a finer grit and leave the machine on for another week. The grits grind away the hard edges of the stones until they are smooth. Finally, you remove the grit, add a fine polishing powder, and run the machine again. The powder gives the stones a shiny finish.

Turquoise

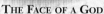

THE FACE OF A GOD

The first recorded use of turquoise dates back to 5000 BC in Mesopotamia (now Iraq), where people used the gemstone to make beads. The Aztec people of North America used turquoise in pendants and ceremonial masks. This mask, made about AD 1500, represents the Aztec god of the wind, Quetzalcoatl.

SHAPES IN THE STONE

Swirling shades of green give malachite a unique beauty. The light green bands are clusters of extremely small crystals. The dark green stripes contain larger crystals. Malachite rarely occurs as big, individual crystals, but it does take on many different shapes. This malachite has a massive habit. Other habits include fibrous, radial (spokelike), and botryoidal (like a bunch of grapes).

JEWELS FROM THE DEEP

Pearls usually grow as small, round stones that are often strung together to make necklaces (above). But people have been known to change the shape of pearls. These Buddha pearls (right) were made by implanting small lead Buddhas into a living mussel. Over several years, the shellfish covered the figures with layers of nacre. This practice began in China in the 12th century.

Malachite

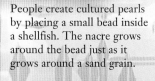

People create cultured pearls by placing a small bead inside a shellfish. The nacre grows around the bead just as it grows around a sand grain.

Sliced in half, a natural pearl would reveal many concentric layers of nacre around a tiny piece of grit. A cultured pearl would contain only a few layers around the bead.

Natural pearl   Cultured pearl

Quartz crystal ball for seeing the future

Eye agate for protecting against the evil eye

Magical Minerals

THE EXTRAORDINARY shapes, colors, and properties of minerals created amazement among early peoples. Our ancestors marveled at smooth, clear quartz crystals that looked like ice but didn't melt, and at stones shaped like needles, grapes, and crosses. They were puzzled by the properties of certain minerals, such as magnetite, which can act like a magnet, and amber, which may contain insects.

Their bewilderment gave rise to many beliefs about minerals, some of which had a basis in fact. For example, quartz was often placed on a person's forehead to cure a fever. This mineral is a good thermal insulator—it retains heat and cold. So, if kept in a cold place, it would feel cool and soothing, just like a cold towel. Native Americans rubbed quartz crystals together during ceremonies to simulate lightning. Quartz does glow when struck or squeezed—a property known as triboluminescence.

Other superstitions relating to minerals have no scientific basis. Some children in Greece wear garnets to keep them safe from drowning. Some farmers in the Middle East tie turquoise to their horses' tails to protect the animals from accidents. And people in many societies still believe that crystals can promote healing and even predict the future.

HOLY CRYSTALS
When the volcano Mount Vesuvius erupted in 1666, crosses rained down on the city of Naples. People called the event a miracle. But the crosses were really crystals of pyroxene that had intergrown at right angles. This process is known as twinning.

Fluorite

HANDS ON
Sweetness and Light

Take a sugar cube into a dark room and squeeze it with a pair of pliers. The cube will glow faintly. Then squeeze harder until the cube shatters. As it breaks, you should see a blue flash.

When you crush the sugar crystals, they break into positively and negatively charged fragments. Energy jumps between the opposite charges, producing sparks. The sparks react with nitrogen in the air to create a bluish flash. This effect—the creation of light by friction—is called triboluminescence. Some minerals, such as quartz and fluorite, are also triboluminescent. Certain materials create a brighter flash because the chemicals they contain also emit light.

CAT'S-EYE GEMS
This gemstone seems to stare right back at you. Its color and stripe of reflected light make it look like the eye of a cat—an effect known as chatoyancy. Several minerals display this effect when cut into round, smooth gems called cabochons. But chatoyant chrysoberyl, shown here, is the truest cat's-eye. The bright yellow line is caused by a row of parallel fibers made of a mineral called rutile, which reflects the light.

FLUORESCENT MINERALS
Fluorescent minerals glow in vibrant colors under ultraviolet light. Other minerals, such as diamond, may continue to glow for a short time after a light is turned off—a trait called phosphorescence. These changes occur because the minerals absorb the light rays and then reradiate them at a different wavelength, producing a visible color.

Word Builders

• People once believed that **jade** could cure kidney pains if applied to the side of the body. The word "jade" comes from the Spanish *piedra de ijada,* which means "stone of the side."
• Ancient Greeks thought that if you put an **amethyst** in your wine, you wouldn't get drunk. Amethyst comes from the Greek word, *amethystos,* which means "not drunken."

That's Amazing!

• The Ancient Egyptians placed emeralds in the throats of mummies to keep them strong in the underworld.
• In the Middle Ages, some doctors believed that if people rubbed themselves with bloodstone and herbs, they could become invisible.
• In the 17th century, an eminent English doctor, William Rowland, claimed that taking crushed garnets would cure heart problems.

Pathfinder

• Rocks display some strange characteristics, too. Turn to pages 24–25.
• Learn more about the odd shapes of minerals on pages 28–29.
• Many unusual gems are used to make jewelry. See pages 44–45.
• Certain minerals have extraordinary properties that we have only recently learned to use. Go to pages 50–51.

Strontianite

BIRTHSTONES

Birthstones can be traced back to ancient times. They may be linked to the twelve gems set in the breastplate of Aaron, a Hebrew priest and brother of the prophet Moses, which represented the 12 tribes of Israel. Later, people began to associate the stones with signs of the zodiac and then with birth months. Today it is still said that your birthstone will bring you good fortune.

JANUARY
Garnet

FEBRUARY
Amethyst

MARCH
Aquamarine

APRIL
Diamond

MAY
Emerald

JUNE
Pearl

JULY
Ruby

AUGUST
Peridot

SEPTEMBER
Sapphire

OCTOBER
Opal

NOVEMBER
Topaz

DECEMBER
Turquoise

RUBY IN MARBLE
Rubies, seen here embedded in marble, are associated with many myths. Burmese warriors believed that if they sewed rubies into their flesh, the gems would protect them in battle. Other peoples claimed that if a ruby turned dark, something bad would happen to its owner.

PIECES OF THE MOON
Certain kinds of feldspar have a pearly white sheen. People thought this looked like the reflection of the moon, so they called these minerals moonstones. The sheen is actually caused by layers of tiny crystals that reflect light. The Roman naturalist Pliny believed that if you held a moonstone up to the stars, it would collect the starlight.

Willemite (green) and calcite (red)

Collecting Rocks and Minerals

THROUGHOUT HISTORY, people have collected rocks and minerals to make useful materials and objects. They have turned them into handy tools. They have gathered them to make homes and other buildings, as well as fuels, ornaments, and jewelry. But some people also collect and study rocks and minerals to learn about our planet. These people are called geologists. You can become a geologist, too. All you need are a few simple tools and a basic knowledge of rocks and minerals. You can study the geology of your area, visit unusual landforms, and gather interesting samples. Eventually, you may create your very own rock and mineral collection.

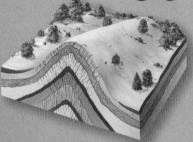

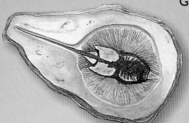

Building Blocks

FOR MILLIONS of years, humans have used rocks to make homes and other buildings. Early humans found shelter in natural caves and soon learned how to carve out their own. Then they began to build shelters using wood, thatch, or mud bricks. But gradually they realized that the strongest, longest-lasting buildings were those made of stone.

As people's skills and knowledge of rocks improved, so did their buildings. The ancient Egyptians learned how to cut limestone from quarries and build enormous pyramids. They also discovered how to use giant slabs of granite to make pavements and walls. The Romans built elegant temples and enormous stadiums using stone such as travertine, a cream-colored porous limestone. In the second century BC, the Chinese began to construct the world's longest wall out of bricks made of granite and other rocks. Many of these ancient structures still stand today.

As time went on, people discovered new materials and techniques. They learned how to make glass out of sand and cut slate tiles for roof shingles. More recently, they began to use steel and concrete (a mixture of water, crushed rock, and cement) to build skyscrapers. Today, you don't need to look far to see rocks being put to good use.

INSIDE STORY
Walled In

The Ch'in ruler Shih Huang Ti, emperor of China, banged his fist on the table. His advisors had just brought him bad news. Mongol horsemen from the north had invaded another village. "We must keep the barbarians out!" he yelled. He then commanded his citizens to reinforce existing village walls and build many new ones. By 210 BC—11 years after the emperor's order—these walls had been joined to form one long wall. Later emperors extended this wall until it encircled the entire kingdom. Today, the Great Wall stretches 2,150 miles (3,461 km) around northern China, and stands 30 feet (9 m) tall in some places.

HANDS ON
Build a Book Bridge

Many early peoples, including the Maya, built bridges, arches, and doorways by stacking stones like steps until the top ones were almost touching. Then they placed another stone on top to form an arch. You can do the same using a pile of books and two chairs.

Place the chairs opposite each other, about 18 inches (46 cm) apart. Build a pile of books on each chair. Place each book so that it is closer to the other chair than the book underneath. When the two piles almost meet, place one last book on top to create an arch or bridge.

SHORE TO SHORE
Different kinds of rocks and minerals were used to build Sydney Harbor Bridge in New South Wales, Australia. The bridge was completed in 1932 and contains 38,000 tons of steel (a mixture of iron and carbon). The pylons are made of granite and the foundations are yellow sandstone.

FROM CAVE TO HIGH-RISE

Through the ages, people have used different types of rocks and minerals to make a wide variety of homes.

TUFF STUFF
Four thousand years ago, people in Cappadocia, Turkey, carved homes in stone pinnacles made of a volcanic rock called tuff. Some of these homes are still in use today.

BRICK BY BRICK
For centuries, some native peoples in the Americas have built homes from adobe bricks. These bricks are made of a mixture of clay (broken-down rock), straw, and water.

Word Builders

• The word **build** comes from the old English term, *byldan*, which comes from another old English word, *bold*, meaning "house" or "dwelling."
• The word **cement** comes from the Latin *caementum*, which means "tough stone."
• The Romans referred to their stadiums as **coliseums**. This name comes from the Latin word *colosseus*, meaning "gigantic."

That's Amazing!

• The Incas, who ruled western South America between 1400 and 1532, constructed huge buildings without mortar. Instead, they cut the stones to fit together perfectly.
• Scientists think that it may have taken prehistoric people a total of 30 million hours to build Stonehenge in southern England. That's equal to spending 24 hours a day in school for 3,424 years!

Pathfinder

• The Mayan and Egyptian pyramids are made of limestone, a sedimentary rock. Find out more about sedimentary rocks on pages 20–21.
• The steel used to build Sydney Harbor Bridge was made from iron ore. Find out how this is done on pages 30–31.

First, the Maya built rough stone walls and filled the cavities behind them with rubble.

Then they built an exterior wall with fine-cut limestone blocks.

PYRAMIDS OF THE WEST

About 2,000 years ago in Mexico and Central America, a people called the Maya used the techniques shown here to create enormous stone temples, some of which contain the tombs of their rulers. Many of these pyramids still stand today.

The exterior wall was covered with fine plaster.

Completed temple.

Workers painted bright colors and designs on the plaster.

Laborers broke rocks into rubble.

Laborers cut the limestone into rectangular blocks.

Stonemasons carved decorative stones to place on the outside of the building.

COUNTRY COTTAGE

In southwest England, people used to build cottages like this one out of a sedimentary stone called oolite. They cut flat pieces of the same rock to make roof tiles.

HIGH-RISE LIVING

Modern apartment buildings house many people on a small area of land. These buildings usually have steel frameworks, concrete floors, and large, steel-framed windows.

Cave painting on rock wall in Spain

Jade carving from China

Pueblo clay pot from the United States

Rock Art

PEOPLE HAVE created art from rocks and minerals since ancient times. Twenty-five thousand years ago, prehistoric humans used colorful dyes made from rocks and minerals to paint scenes on cave walls. Five thousand years ago, the ancient Egyptians carved jewelry from a variety of minerals, including quartz, obsidian, lapis lazuli, and gold. Later, the ancient Romans and Greeks sculpted magnificent works of art from blocks of marble. Today, people flock to museums to admire this art.

But rock art is not just about beauty. Ancient artworks that have survived for centuries tell us about our ancestors' lifestyles. Cave paintings show us which animals the first humans hunted. Metal tools and weapons reveal how people worked and fought. Ancient jewelry tells us which minerals a people valued most. Sculptures preserve artistic perceptions for new generations.

Today, we continue to use rocks and minerals in art. We fashion jewelry from precious metals and gems. We create sculptures from stones and metals. Modern technology makes it simpler for us to create rock art than it was for our ancestors. For example, advanced techniques make it easier to extract stone, gems, and metals from Earth's crust. We know how to mix metals together to make them stronger and how to cut a gemstone to make it shine brighter. Thousands of years from now, our rock art may well help future societies understand how we lived.

CROWN JEWELS
This spectacular crown was made in 1605 for the coronation of Prince Stephen Bocksay of Transylvania, in eastern Europe. It is made of gold and inset with rubies, emeralds, turquoise, and pearls.

MODERN ROCK ART
Many artists use metals to make modern sculptures. This artist is polishing a sculpture made of bronze, a mixture of the metals copper and tin.

PAINTING WITH ROCKS
The Navajo people of North America use powdered rocks to create pictures. First, they color sand using dyes obtained from rocks, minerals, plants, and ashes. Then they gently pour the sand onto the ground to create traditional designs. Originally, the Navajo made these paintings for healing ceremonies. After the ceremony, they destroyed the painting.

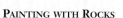

The mask is made of solid gold.

MASK OF TUTANKHAMEN
This spectacular death mask was made for Tutankhamen, an Egyptian king, or pharaoh. He began his reign in 1361 BC at age nine, and died mysteriously at age 18. His subjects mummified his body and put this mask over his head and shoulders. Then they placed the body inside a pyramid. This tomb remained sealed until 1922, when it was discovered by archeologist Howard Carter.

The Egyptians didn't have enough lapis lazuli to make these stripes on the hood, so they used blue glass instead.

The collar is encrusted with lapis lazuli, quartz, and green feldspar.

Word Builders

Gems are measured in **carats**. The word "carat" comes from the Greek word *keration,* which means "carob bean." At one time, gems were weighed against piles of carob beans. One carat is roughly the weight of a carob bean—0.007 ounce (0.2 g).

That's Amazing!

• Cave paintings found in Namibia in Africa may be the world's oldest rock art. They are about 27,500 years old.
• In ancient Egypt, there were hundreds of royal tombs like that of Tutankhamen. But almost every one was robbed within 10 years of being sealed.

Pathfinder

• Before they can be used for jewelry, stones have to be polished. Find out how to do this on page 37.
• Gems are crystals of minerals. Learn more about crystals on pages 28–29.
• Gold is a precious native metal. Take a look at two giant gold nuggets and find out how they formed on pages 32–33.

INSIDE STORY

All in a Day's Work

Gem cutter Lazare Kaplan held what looked like a glass egg. But this was no egg. It was the Jonker diamond, a 726-carat gem discovered in 1934 by Jacobus Jonker in South Africa. Two years later, the owners hired Kaplan to cut the diamond into smaller ones. Lazare etched a groove into the gem. Sweat ran down his brow. If he split the stone in the wrong place, it could shatter into tiny bits. Holding his breath, he placed a steel rule in the groove and gave it a sharp tap. CRACK! The diamond split perfectly in half. Lazare breathed a sigh of relief. Eventually, he cut the halves into 12 diamonds, one of which was sold for one million dollars.

The eyes contain quartz and obsidian, and the eyebrows and eyelids are lapis lazuli.

THE PLAY OF LIGHT

Gem cutters make gems sparkle. They grind angled cuts, or facets, on the surface of a stone. Light enters each facet and bounces around inside before shooting back out. Different cuts create a different dance of light. Here are some diagrams of common gem cuts (left) with examples of cut gems (right).

Table cut

Emerald cut

Round brilliant cut

Pear-shaped brilliant cut

Heart-shaped brilliant cut

Cabochon (smoothly polished—no cuts)

Geologist's microscope

Geological map and compass

The Keys to the Rocks

ONCE HUMANS became aware of the value of rocks, they started to ask questions. Where do rocks come from? Do rocks grow? To find answers to these questions, people began to study rocks. But their answers weren't always correct. The Greek philosopher Aristotle taught that minerals rose from vapors inside Earth. And only 200 years ago, most scientists believed that the world was just 6,000 years old.

Today, people who study rocks are called geologists, and they know a little more. Geologists are like detectives. They search the world for clues to Earth's past. Because rocks are gradually yet continually changing, much of the evidence has disappeared. But geologists use a range of modern techniques and devices to retrieve what is left. They drill into seafloors to look at ancient sediments. They monitor earthquakes to learn what happens under ground. And they use microscopes to examine minerals and fossils. They can even create computer models that simulate geological processes on Earth.

Their detective work has paid off. Today we know that Earth is about 4.8 billion years old. We have a good idea of how it formed and why it continues to change. And, thanks to one intrepid geologist, we have even learned about the geology of our nearest neighbor, the Moon.

THE BIG PICTURE

By adjusting the color range of a satellite image, scientists can map the locations of different rocks. This satellite image shows part of the Himalaya Mountains in Tibet, China. Most of the rocks are granites, which appear as an orangey brown color. The bluish patches are sedimentary rocks.

INSIDE STORY

The First Geologist on the Moon

On December 11, 1972, geologist Harrison "Jack" Schmitt stepped onto the Moon's rough surface. As part of the *Apollo 17* mission, Jack was the first geologist on the Moon. He would also be the last, so he knew his job had special meaning. As Jack said later, the Moon was "a geologist's paradise." He collected many rock samples, including breccia and other igneous rocks. Scientists were able to learn a great deal about the Moon from these rocks. They found out that it had experienced lava eruptions, earthquakes, and many asteroid impacts. Jack's lunar rock hunt had paid off.

GEOLOGISTS AT WORK

Wherever there's a geological puzzle, you'll find scientists searching for the answers. Their curiosity can take them to the tops of high mountains and deep into caves. These geologists are braving intense heat to study a fiery lava tube in Hawaii, U.S.A.

MAPPING THE OCEAN FLOOR

Vast mountain ranges, deep canyons, and immense plains lie deep beneath the ocean. Scientists use a variety of instruments and techniques to study these formations.

By figuring how long it takes sound waves to bounce back to a ship from the seafloor, scientists can measure the depths of valleys and the heights of mountains.

Word Builders

• The study of the history and structure of Earth is known as **geology.** The word "geology" comes from the Greek words *geo,* meaning "earth," and *logos,* meaning "study of."
• **Microscope** comes from two Greek words: *mikros,* meaning "small," and *skopein,* meaning "to look at."

That's Amazing!

• Ocean ridges cover 23 percent of Earth's surface. That's almost as much as all the continents combined.
• If you were to dig 10 miles (16 km) down under the southern Rocky Mountains in the U.S.A., you would find the same rock that lies at the bottom of the Grand Canyon—Vishnu Schist.

Pathfinder

• How do geologists study Earth's interior? Learn more on pages 10–11.
• Earth may be nearly five billion years old, but in geological terms, humans have just arrived. Turn to pages 16–17.
• Interested in becoming a geologist? Get a head start on pages 52–53.
• Fascinated by fossils? See pages 60–61.

HANDS ON
Making a Core Sample

To study rock layers, scientists take core samples from Earth's crust. They do this by drilling into the ground with a hollow drill. You can make your own core sample using modeling clay and a straw.

❶ Roll several pieces of different-colored clay into flat pieces. Place them one on top of the other to form colorful layers.

❷ Take a strong, wide drinking straw and slowly push it through the layers of clay.

❸ Pull the straw out, then ask an adult to cut it open. Inside you'll find your clay core sample.

RECREATING THE PAST

By studying fossils and rocks in the walls of the Grand Canyon, geologists can paint a picture of the canyon's history. This history dates back more than two billion years. To follow the history, read the labels from the bottom of the canyon up. The numbers on the right show when each part of the canyon formed.

MILLIONS OF YEARS AGO

Kaibab Limestone: contains the remains of sea creatures — 265

Toroweap Sandstone: formed from sand deposited by a sea — 270

Coconino Sandstone: the remains of a vast desert — 275

Hermit Shale: formed from silt deposited by a river system — 280

Supai Group: sandstone ledges and slopes formed from mud and sand deposited by rivers and oceans — 300

Redwall Limestone: contains the remains of later marine creatures — 340

Temple Butte Limestone: formed as more creatures lived and died in the warm sea — 375

Muav Limestone: formed from the remains of early sea creatures — 520

Bright Angel Shale: formed from muds and silts deposited in the sea as it flooded the land — 540

Tapeats Sandstone: the remains of a beach that formed as a sea moved in over the old eroded mountains — 560

Zoroaster Granite: formed when magma pushed into the Vishnu Schist and cooled very slowly

Vishnu Schist: a metamorphic rock that formed part of a huge mountain range. The range was created two billion years ago when two continents collided.

— 2,000

Using minisubmarines, scientists can visit ocean ridges (undersea mountain ranges). Many contain "black smokers"—vents where boiling water rises out of the crust.

Computers can be used to map the seafloor. This map shows the Mid-Atlantic ocean ridge. The highest parts of the ridge are red, and the lowest parts are blue.

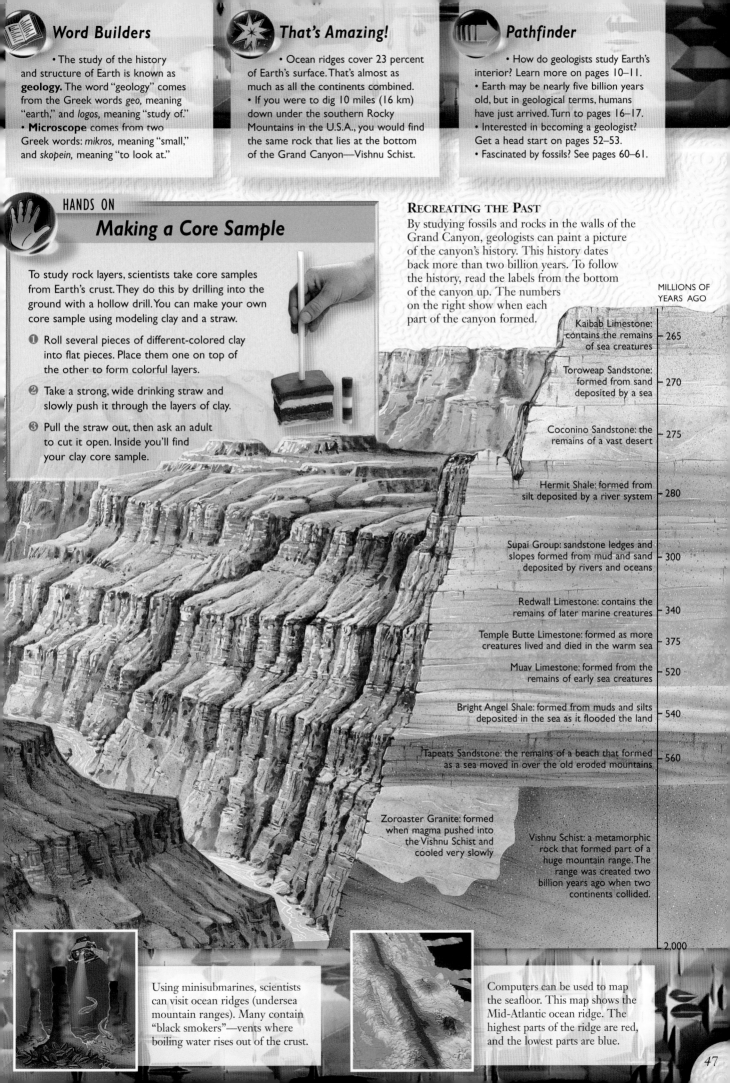

Rocks to Burn

ROCKS HOLD the power to fuel the world. Coal, oil, gas and other energy resources lie buried in layers of sedimentary rocks. If it weren't for these fuels, you couldn't ride in a car, fly in a plane, or stay warm in the winter.

One of the most widely used fuels is coal. We burn it to produce heat and energy. Coal consists of the remains of ancient swamp plants. As the plants decay in mud, they turn into peat, a substance that looks like moist tobacco. Sometimes, sedimentary rocks form on top of the peat, crushing it with their weight. The squashed peat then turns into a dark brown rock called lignite. As more layers of rock press down on it, lignite becomes bituminous coal. Under extreme pressure, bituminous coal changes into anthracite, a hard, shiny, black coal. The more coal is squeezed, the harder it becomes and the more energy it releases when burned.

Unfortunately, our supplies of coal, oil, and gas are running out. Because of this, people have tried to find other sources of energy. One type—called nuclear energy—comes from uranium-rich rocks. Uranium is a heavy element with big atoms. When the atoms are split apart, energy is released. This energy is turned into power at nuclear power stations.

SOMETHING IN THE AIR

When people burn oil, coal, or gas, it creates a type of pollution called smog. Smog is a mix of dust, smoke, and gases that makes it hard for some people to breathe.

MODERN MINING

For centuries, people have descended far below Earth's surface to dig coal out of sedimentary rocks. Today, machines do most of the digging. The method shown here is now used in most coal mines. It is known as continuous mining.

To reach the coal face, miners take the downcast shaft. Fans at the top of the shaft supply them with air.

The miners dig tunnels through the rock. They use metal pillars to support the roof.

The miners descend to the coal face in a metal elevator known as a cage.

UNDER THE SEA

Oil and gas form when the decayed remains of ocean animals are crushed between layers of rock.

Microscopic sea creatures die and fall to the ocean floor. Over millions of years, layers of mud and silt slowly cover the sea creatures and turn into sedimentary rocks.

The rock layers continue to pile up on top of the dead sea creatures. As the pressure from the rocks increases, the sea creatures slowly turn into oil and gas.

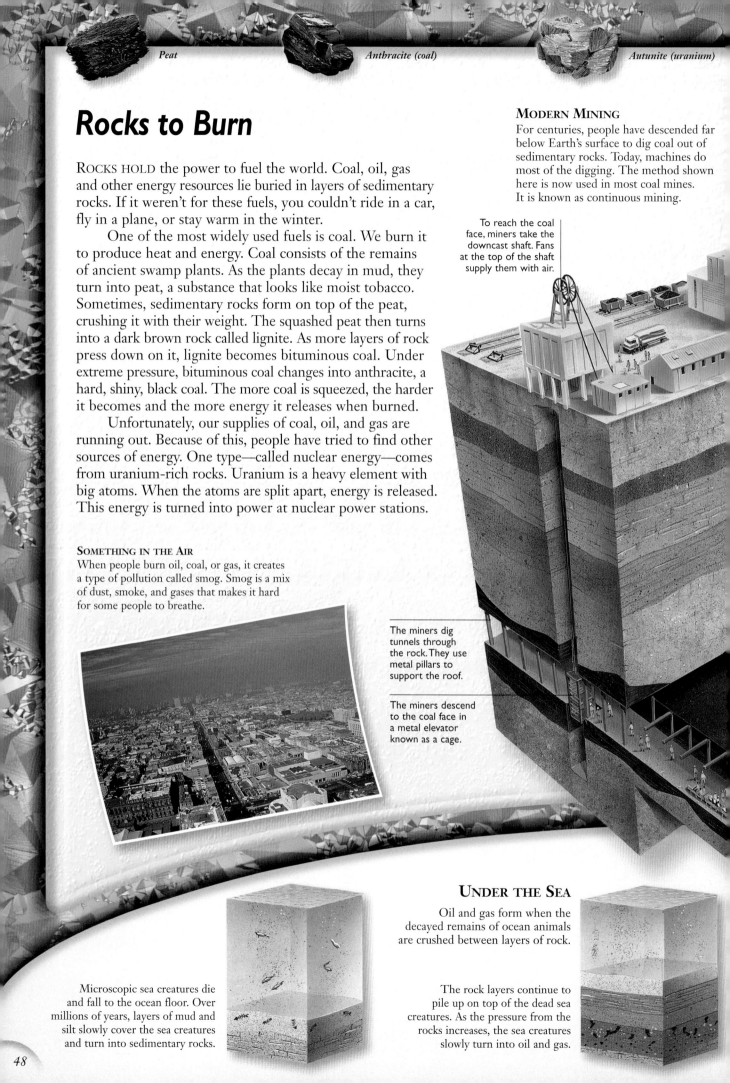

Word Builders

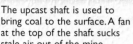

• Oil and gas are **petroleum** products. The word "petroleum" comes from the Latin words *petro,* meaning "stone," and *oleum,* meaning "oil."
• **Uranium** is named after the Greek god of the heavens, Uranus.

That's Amazing!

An underground coal seam on Mount Wingen in southeastern Australia has been on fire for 5,000 years. Smoke continually seeps out of the mountain, which is too hot to walk on. The name "Wingen" comes from an Aboriginal word meaning "fire."

Pathfinder

• Coal is a type of sedimentary rock. To find out more about these rocks, turn to pages 20–21.
• Did you know that coal and diamonds are made of the same material—an element called carbon? To learn more about diamonds, turn to pages 34–35.

The upcast shaft is used to bring coal to the surface. A fan at the top of the shaft sucks stale air out of the mine.

Coal is loaded onto rail cars for transportation.

INSIDE STORY
The Breaker Boy

My name is Paul. I work in a coal mine in Scranton, Pennsylvania. That's in the United States. My job is to split the slate apart from the coal using a hammer. That's why I'm called a "breaker boy." I work long days and often don't get home until after dark. The coal is dirty. Black dust covers my skin and gets inside my nose and mouth. My boss told me that the coal we find helps power new steam locomotives. I guess that makes my job important. But I can't wait to be a miner. Miners get to buy explosives from the company store and blow up rock to search for more coal. Maybe I'll get promoted after my birthday. I'll be 11 on May 6, 1894.

The coal is taken to the surface in a large metal container called a skip.

The broken coal falls onto a conveyor belt that takes it to the upcast shaft.

A machine called a cutting head tears into the coal with its sharp-toothed wheel.

OFFSHORE OIL
Geologists use offshore oil platforms to explore ocean sediments for oil and gas. From a single platform like this one, workers can drill as many as 50 different wells and collect millions of barrels of oil each day. Most oil platforms remain at sea for about 25 years, though one was in use for 60 years.

The oil and gas rise through the rock layers. They pass through porous rocks, such as sandstone, but are blocked by impermeable (nonporous) rocks, such as shale.

Under the right conditions, the oil and gas collect in a reservoir under the impermeable rocks, with the gas on top of the oil. Humans drill into reservoirs to remove the fuels.

Chips Off the Old Block

IN RECENT YEARS, information from geologists and advances in technology have helped us to find new uses for rocks and minerals. For example, in the early 1880s, two scientist brothers found that a common mineral called quartz produces an electric current when squeezed. Today, quartz clocks and watches use this property to keep time. Quartz is also the raw material for silicon, a substance that helps energy flow through electronic instruments. Without silicon, you wouldn't be able to play electronic games or use a computer, telephone, television, or stereo.

Modern technology has also created super-strong materials from substances extracted from rocks and minerals. By combining carbon fibers obtained from petroleum with a plastic resin, scientists can make a strong, flexible material that is commonly referred to as graphite. Manufacturers use this substance in everything from tennis rackets to skis and fishing rods. Scientists have also learned how to use oil extracted from rocks to make other synthetic fibers, plastics, paint, and fuels.

Rocks and minerals have even helped humans travel to outer space. The metal titanium, for example, can be mixed with other metals to produce a strong, lightweight material that doesn't rust. This makes it ideal for building spacecraft.

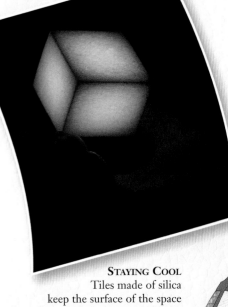

STAYING COOL
Tiles made of silica keep the surface of the space shuttle cool when it reenters Earth's atmosphere. These tiles insulate heat so well that you can hold one by the edges even though the interior is 2,300° Fahrenheit (1,260° C).

The payload doors are made of a mixture of carbon, graphite, and fiberglass that is 23 percent lighter than aluminum.

Kevlar window shades covered with silver tape protect astronauts from sun glare.

The nose cone is reinforced with carbon to resist intense heat.

The windows have a scratch-resistant diamond coating.

INSIDE STORY

A Tight Squeeze

In 1880, two chemist brothers, Jacques and Pierre Curie, decided to perform an experiment. With a special saw, they cut a thin slice of quartz. Then they attached a sheet of tin to either side of the slice of quartz. Next, they used a machine to squeeze the tin tightly against the mineral. This pressure created a small flow of electric charges in the quartz. The brothers were delighted with this result. But it was only later, in the 1920s, that scientists realized that this phenomenon—known as piezoelectricity—could be used to keep time. Today, almost all clocks and watches are operated by tiny, pulsing quartz crystals.

COUNTING THE HOURS
Charged by a battery, the quartz crystal in a watch vibrates 32,786 times per second. A circuit counts the vibrations and sorts them into seconds, minutes, and hours.

DIAMOND HARD
A scratch-resistant coating made of diamonds protects these ordinary sunglasses. This lens coating was originally developed to protect the windows on the space shuttle.

Word Builders

- **Graphite,** a soft, black form of the element carbon, is used to make pencils. The word comes from the Greek *graphein,* meaning "to write or draw."
- **Piezoelectricity** comes from the Greek *piezein,* meaning "to squeeze."
- **Titanium** is named after Greek gods called Titans, who were feared for their great strength and size.

That's Amazing!

- A silicon chip the size of an average shirt button can contain hundreds of thousands of electrical components.
- Ninety-five percent of titanium mined today is used to create a white pigment that makes paper, paint, and plastics brilliant white.

Pathfinder

- Quartz, one of the most common minerals, is found in many rocks. Learn more about quartz on pages 54–55.
- Diamonds form deep inside Earth's crust. See pages 34–35 to find out how they get to the surface.

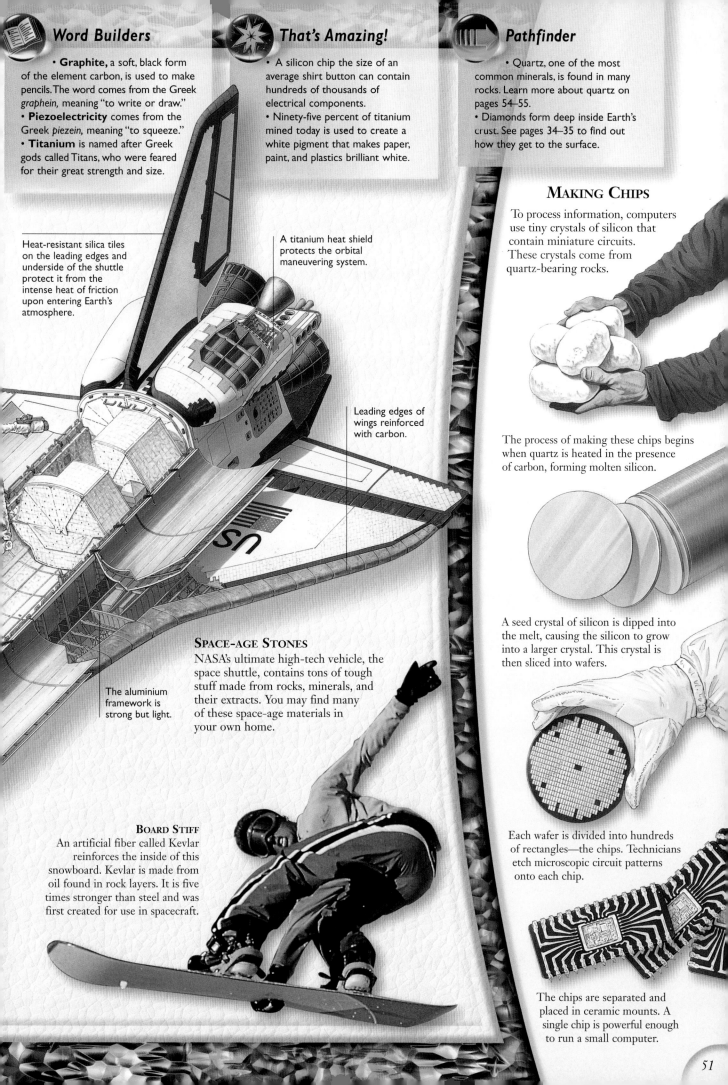

Heat-resistant silica tiles on the leading edges and underside of the shuttle protect it from the intense heat of friction upon entering Earth's atmosphere.

A titanium heat shield protects the orbital maneuvering system.

Leading edges of wings reinforced with carbon.

The aluminium framework is strong but light.

MAKING CHIPS

To process information, computers use tiny crystals of silicon that contain miniature circuits. These crystals come from quartz-bearing rocks.

The process of making these chips begins when quartz is heated in the presence of carbon, forming molten silicon.

A seed crystal of silicon is dipped into the melt, causing the silicon to grow into a larger crystal. This crystal is then sliced into wafers.

Each wafer is divided into hundreds of rectangles—the chips. Technicians etch microscopic circuit patterns onto each chip.

The chips are separated and placed in ceramic mounts. A single chip is powerful enough to run a small computer.

SPACE-AGE STONES

NASA's ultimate high-tech vehicle, the space shuttle, contains tons of tough stuff made from rocks, minerals, and their extracts. You may find many of these space-age materials in your own home.

BOARD STIFF

An artificial fiber called Kevlar reinforces the inside of this snowboard. Kevlar is made from oil found in rock layers. It is five times stronger than steel and was first created for use in spacecraft.

Magnifying glass   *Brushes*   *Pliers*

Be a Rock Hound

YOU CAN COLLECT and study rocks just like the experts. It's easy to get started, and you don't need much equipment. Gather together a rock hammer, a sample-collecting bag, a notebook, a pen, safety glasses, pliers, some newspaper, and a field guide to rocks and minerals. Now you're ready to go. Don't forget to pack a snack before you head off.

     You can search for rocks and minerals almost anywhere. Try your backyard first. If you don't have one or don't find much there, look along the banks of streams or near rocky outcrops. Always use caution. Watch for falling rocks and stay out of dangerous places such as quarries. It's safer, and usually more fun, to hunt for rocks with a friend. Ask permission before you look for rocks on private property. When you're there, act like a guest. Only pick up rocks that will enhance your collection. Be a rock hound, not a rock hog.

     When you find a rock you like, note the location, the date, and who found it. You can trim off the parts of the rock you don't want with a hammer or pliers, but make sure you protect your eyes with safety glasses. Wrap the rock in newspaper and put it in your bag. Once you get home, clean and number the rock. Then transfer the information about your find to an index card. Now your rock is ready for display.

A CLOSER LOOK
You can use a magnifying glass to take a close look at rocks. Is the rock bumpy or smooth? Can you identify the minerals in the rock?

Write the details of your find on an index card. Note where and when you found it.

A small set of shelves can make an excellent display case for rock and mineral samples.

HANDS ON
Make a Display Case

You can make a simple rock and mineral display case out of an egg carton. Simply place wads of cotton or tissue paper in each compartment. This kind of box is ideal for displaying small specimens. It's also handy for carrying your rocks around.

     For a larger display box, find a big, low-sided cardboard box. You can make compartments with smaller boxes, or with strips of heavy card. Simply cut the strips of card to fit the length and width of the box. Then cut slits in the strips so that you can slot them together.

PREPARING SPECIMENS
When you bring your specimens home, carefully unpack them from their newspaper wrapping. Then prepare them as follows.

First, clean your rock using a toothbrush or other soft brush, and soap and water. If your specimen is delicate, you should skip this step.

Word Builders

• People who search for rocks and minerals are known as **rock hounds** because they hunt rocks just as a hunter's hounds pursue animals.
• The rocks and minerals you collect in the field are known as **specimens**. The word "specimen" comes from the Latin *specere,* which means "to look at."
• **Museum** comes from the Greek *mouseion,* which means "place of study."

That's Amazing!

• People started collecting rocks at least 2.3 million years ago. That's when ancestors of humans first began to use rocks as tools.
• The Natural History Museum in London, England, has one of the largest rock collections in the world. It contains 350,000 minerals and 100,000 rocks.

Pathfinder

• Learn how to identify rocks and minerals on pages 54–55.
• What's the difference between a rock and a mineral? Find out on pages 28–29.
• For more tips on where to go rock hunting, turn to pages 56–57.
• Keen on beachcombing? Go to pages 58–59 for advice on seashore collecting.

PUTTING ON A SHOW

You can arrange your collection just as museums do. First, use a field guide to identify and label your rocks. Then organize them into groups. You can sort them according to where you found them, or into igneous, sedimentary, and metamorphic types. Keep fragile specimens in boxes or drawers. But don't hide your rocks. You worked hard to find them, so display them with pride.

Study your rock carefully with a magnifying glass. Compare your specimen to the photos in a field guide of rocks and minerals.

INSIDE STORY

Collector Extraordinaire

Australian amateur rock hound Albert Chapman created one of the world's best private mineral collections. As a child, Albert started picking up rocks at the harbor near his home. Later he traveled the country in search of unique specimens. Albert liked to visit mines, where he sometimes bought rocks from miners. He traded the rocks with geologists, museums, and other collectors. But the rocks he found himself were his favorites. "Anything you collect for yourself is a thrill," he would say. Albert couldn't get enough of rocks and minerals. "I like the way they come out of the ground," he explained. "I like their colors and forms." Albert died in 1996. But his magnificent collection is now on display in the Australian Museum in Sydney for all to see.

LEARNING FROM THE EXPERTS

You can learn more about the geology of your area by visiting your local museum. Museums usually have big glass cases filled with interesting rocks and minerals. You might recognize some that are in your collection. Others may be unique specimens or come from other countries.

You can protect fragile rocks and minerals by keeping them in a drawer.

Divide the drawer into compartments using strips of cardboard, or put each sample into its own box.

Next, carefully paint a small white spot on the bottom of your rock or mineral using white model paint or correction fluid. Leave it to dry.

Write a number on the white spot. Put the same number on an index card. Use the card to note important details about the rock and where you found it.

Name That Rock

JUST LIKE PEOPLE, rocks and minerals possess certain traits that make them stand out from the crowd. For example, you can identify minerals by examining how shiny, dense, and hard they are. The colors, textures, and types of minerals in a rock may tell you how it formed. By learning to recognize these characteristics, you can become a top rock spotter.

When you find an interesting rock, look at it carefully. Is it made up of a single mineral or many minerals? More than 600 basic rock types exist, so if it's a rock, you should start by narrowing the field. Try to work out which kind of rock you have—sedimentary, igneous, or metamorphic. Certain clues, such as the shape, size, alignment, and distribution of the crystals, will tip you off. For instance, most intrusive igneous rocks have large- to medium-sized mineral grains that you can see without a magnifying glass.

If the rock contains large crystals, the minerals can sometimes be identified. A number of simple tests can help. For example, quartz and calcite crystals may look similar. But quartz is harder and will scratch the calcite when the two are rubbed together. Compare your observations and test results to the information in a field guide. With a little practice, you'll soon learn to put names to rock faces.

IDENTIFYING ROCKS

When you find an unidentified rock, pick it up and study it closely. How heavy is it for its size? What color is it? Can you make out details such as large crystals, bands of different-colored stone, or clumps of pebbles? All of these features will help you make the first step in rock identification—deciding whether the rock is sedimentary, igneous, or metamorphic.

This sedimentary rock is called conglomerate. It consists of pebbles of milky quartz surrounded by smaller fragments of sand, clay, and iron oxide.

Conglomerate

Milky quartz

SEDIMENTARY ROCK

Sedimentary rocks may have distinct layers made up of grains of different sizes, or look like a mixture of different rocks. They are seldom shiny and seldom contain well-defined crystals. If you can see fossils in a rock, it is probably sedimentary.

IGNEOUS ROCK

Igneous rocks can contain large, well-defined crystals, appear smooth and glassy, or fall somewhere in between. But, in general, they all have a uniform texture and even distribution of colors.

Granite

Feldspar

Quartz

You can easily spot the large quartz, feldspar, and mica crystals in this piece of granite. Other igneous rocks, such as basalt, have fine crystals that can be seen only with a magnifying glass.

Mica

INSIDE STORY

He Wrote the Book on Minerals

People have collected rocks for thousands of years. But a practical book about minerals didn't appear until 1546. It was called *De Natura Fossilium* and was written by a German scientist named Georgius Agricola. Agricola wrote the book while working as a doctor near a major mining center in Germany. Agricola visited the mines every day and gained a wide knowledge of rocks. He was the first scientist to describe minerals by their form, color, hardness, and luster—the very properties we use to identify minerals today.

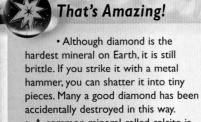

Word Builders

• The **Mohs scale** of hardness is named for its inventor, an Austrian mineralogist called Friedrich Mohs. He devised the scale in 1822.
• Rock hounds are often confused by a mineral called **apatite**. It often looks like other minerals, such as aquamarine, olivine, and fluorite. Apatite takes its name from the Greek word *apate*, which means "deceit."

That's Amazing!

• Although diamond is the hardest mineral on Earth, it is still brittle. If you strike it with a metal hammer, you can shatter it into tiny pieces. Many a good diamond has been accidentally destroyed in this way.
• A common mineral called calcite is a master of disguise. It is found in over 300 different crystal forms—more than any other mineral.

Pathfinder

• Learn about the fiery origins of igneous rocks on pages 18–19.
• You can make your own sedimentary layers. Turn to page 20.
• Find out how heat and pressure create metamorphic rocks on pages 22–23.
• The habit of a mineral may be a clue to its identity. See pages 28–29.

Banded gneiss

This gneiss (pronounced "nice") has a coarse texture and folded layers of light and dark minerals. Gneiss can look similar to granite, but it commonly contains layers of crystals rather than scattered pieces.

Feldspar

METAMORPHIC ROCK
Many metamorphic rocks contain bands of light and dark minerals or layers of flaky minerals. This is called foliation. Other metamorphic rocks, such as marble, have a more even color and are made up of small, interlocking crystals.

Biotite

Quartz

MOHS SCALE

The Mohs scale of hardness uses 10 minerals that range from the softest to the hardest to help determine the hardness of other minerals. If you scratch quartz against an unknown mineral and it leaves a mark, you know that the mystery mineral is softer than quartz. You can also use the items on the right-hand side to test for hardness in the same way.

1. TALC
2. GYPSUM
2.5. Fingernail
3. CALCITE
3.5. Copper coin
4. FLUORITE
5. APATITE
5.5. Glass
6. ORTHOCLASE (A TYPE OF FELDSPAR)
6.5. Steel knife
7. QUARTZ
8. TOPAZ
8.5. Emery board
9. CORUNDUM
10. DIAMOND

HANDS ON

Test Cases

If you find a piece of a mineral, you can identify it using these steps.

❶ Make notes on the mineral's appearance. What color is it? Is it transparent (you can see through it) or opaque (you can't)? Is it shiny or dull? What habit (shape) does it have?

❷ Rub your mineral against an unglazed white porcelain tile (the back of a ceramic tile will do). This is called a streak test. What color streak does the mineral leave? You can take a look at some examples at the top of the opposite page.

❸ Hold the mineral in your hand or weigh it on scales. Some minerals are much heavier than others of the same size. For example, sulfur is light, but a piece of pyrite the same size is much heavier.

❹ Use the information on the right to conduct a hardness test. (Be careful not to damage the specimen.) What is the hardness of your mineral?

To determine the type of mineral, compare your test results to the measurements for color and luster, weight, streak-test color, and hardness in a good field guide.

Sulfur

Pyrite

*Hard hat and
safety goggles*

*Bag for carrying
samples*

*Hammer
and chisels*

Take to the Hills

ROCKS ABOUND in hills, mountains, and other upland areas. Here you'll find natural landforms such as jagged mountain peaks, craggy outcrops, and deep river valleys. You'll also come across human-made features, such as road and rail cuts, that reveal interesting rocks and minerals.

Road cuts are great places for studying rocks. They appear whenever a construction crew blasts through a hillside to make room for a new road. A fresh road cut lets you look at rocks that aren't covered by plants or altered by exposure to the elements. You might be able to take a close look at layers of sedimentary rock, for instance. Each layer will have its own color and minerals. A road cut in igneous or metamorphic rocks may have mineral veins cutting through it or nice, large crystals. If you want to get a close look at a road cut, be sure you obey the road rules and keep away from traffic.

Certain higher-ground features provide happy hunting for rock hounds. For example, rivers and streams cut through the land, carrying off rocks and minerals. You can then find excellent specimens washed up on their banks. Erosion and uplift can expose rocks that are still rooted in the ground. These are called outcrops. Usually, the rock is made from strong minerals—a fine addition to any collection.

WINDOWS ON THE PAST
Road cuts expose rock layers and allow us to study the landscape's past. This one in Australia shows two faults in sedimentary rock layers. The faults were created by movement in Earth's crust.

Rivers create V-shaped valleys. With renewed uplift or along faults and joints, gorges may form.

Mountain peaks often have little vegetation, so you can take a close look at the rocks.

Road cuts reveal rock layers and interesting formations.

HANDS ON

Field Notes

When you go out into the field, always take a notebook so you can record your observations and discoveries. Choose a notebook with a hard cover—preferably one that's waterproof.

Each time you find an interesting geological feature (like the ones shown below), draw a rough map to record its location. Then try to sketch the feature. For example, if you are studying a road cut, draw any rock layers, faults, or joints. If you can identify the layers, label the rock types. You may also want to take photographs of particularly interesting or unusual landforms. Eventually your notebook will provide you with a fascinating record of the geology of your area.

Folded rock layers

Joints

WRINKLES IN THE ROCKS

Look out for these landforms when rock hunting in the hills. They are signs of major events in the history of any landscape. The illustrations show you how to recognize each feature and what to look for when you find it.

A fold is a bend in rock layers formed when the rock was crumpled by plate movements. You can often see folds in road and rail cuts. If the layers fold upward, it's called an anticline. If the layers crumple downward, it's a syncline. A crack in the rock is called a joint.

📖 Word Builders

• Mountains, valleys, and plains make up a landscape's **topography**. The word topography comes from the Greek words *topos,* meaning "place," and *graphein,* meaning "to write."
• A **drumlin** is an oval hill created by a glacier. The name comes from the Irish word *druim,* meaning "back" or "ridge."
• An **esker** is a long, narrow hill formed by a glacier. The name comes from the Irish word *escir,* meaning "ridge."

✴ That's Amazing!

• During the last ice age, a glacier cut a valley 2,000 feet (610 m) deep into the Rocky Mountains in the U.S.A.
• The tiny country of San Marino in Italy is upside down! Scientists have worked out that millions of years ago the rock layers under the country were overturned by plate movements.

🏛 Pathfinder

• Glaciers are giant rivers of ice. Find out more on pages 14–15.
• Road and rail cuts can reveal rock layers that may contain fossils. Find out about fossils on pages 60–61.
• People have often found precious metals such as gold and silver in rivers. Learn more on pages 32–33.

A GEOLOGICAL SURVEY

From a hilltop, you can survey the countryside for prime rock-hunting locations. Look for road or railway cuts that expose layers of rock. Search mountainsides for rivers that carry rocks and pebbles. Scan the horizon for U-shaped valleys carved by glaciers. And don't forget to inspect other, more obvious features such as cliffs and outcrops.

🔍 INSIDE STORY

Layers of History

By studying the rocks along slices and holes that people had cut into the land, William Smith became the first scientist to understand the significance of rock layers. Smith worked as a surveyor in England during the 1790s. While examining coal mines and canal banks in different parts of the country, he noticed that they contained similar rock layers. By comparing fossils in the layers, Smith worked out that the rocks always appeared in the same order. From this, he correctly concluded that they had built up on top of each other, so that the oldest rocks were at the bottom and the youngest at the top. Smith's discoveries allowed him to create the first geological map of England. They also provided other geologists with a whole new way of looking at landscapes.

Valleys gouged by glaciers have a distinctive U shape.

Resistant rocks protrude from softer ground that has been worn down.

Cliff faces may contain layers, folds, and faults. They are also good spots for finding fossils.

Rail cuts and quarries reveal rock that may have been hidden for centuries.

ROUND THE BEND

As a river rounds a corner, it leaves pebbles and stones on the shore. A river bend is therefore a great spot to find rock and mineral samples. Use caution when hunting near rivers. Better yet, ask an adult to come along.

Glaciers literally sculpt the landscape. They may leave mounds of debris called moraines or eskers, or create new features called drumlins or hanging valleys. A hanging valley indicates the presence of a smaller glacier next to the main one.

Hanging valley

Esker

Drumlin

Moraine

A fault is a special kind of crack in the land. It forms when the crust is stretched or compressed by plate movements, causing land to collapse or rise. Signs of faults include layers that don't line up and clifflike structures called scarps.

Scarp

Joint

Fault

Large, flat mica beach pebbles

Flat slate beach pebbles

Rounded granite pebbles

Fine quartzite beach pebbles

Coast Watch

THE COAST is a great place for geology watchers. Water and wind constantly sculpt the coastline into fantastic landforms. Pounding waves carve arches, caves, platforms, and sea stacks out of cliff faces. Heavily laden rivers dump silt, gravel, and mud on the shore. Gusting winds pile sand into massive dunes. All this happens bit by bit, although you can sometimes see huge changes after a big storm.

These natural forces also polish pebbles, stones, and shells into ready-made samples for your collections. They may also bring you specimens from other locations. For example, rivers transport pebbles and stones from far upstream. And large waves and strong ocean currents may deposit rocks and sand from other beaches.

Because the coastline is constantly changing, geologists who study these environments must stay on their toes. Rivers carry heavy loads of sediment that can pile up and alter a current's course. This can put boats in danger. Erosion can sweep away fragile cliffs. And when cliffs crumble, nearby houses may collapse, too. But these changes can also be fascinating, and not just for geologists. They are continually revealing new mineral samples, rock formations, and ancient fossils—evidence of Earth's most powerful forces.

A WHALE OF A ROCK

In Western Australia, water spurts from this blowhole as if the rock were a whale. The hole formed when pounding surf cut through weak rock at the bottom of the cliff and tunneled up to the surface. Now when a big wave crashes against the cliff, its weight forces water up through the hole.

Blowholes form when the sea tunnels through a headland.

Erosion causes cliffs to collapse, forming piles of rock.

Sea cliffs may contain interesting rock layers and fossils.

Sea stacks are the remains of headlands.

Waves gnaw at cliffs, creating sea caves and arches.

WORN BY THE WAVES

Huge mounds of rock and pillars called sea stacks form where waves claw at the shore. The process may take thousands of years.

Erosion often creates formations called headlands, which jut out into the water. Waves pound the headlands, scooping out caves from areas of softer rock.

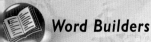
Word Builders

• **Coast** comes from the Latin word *costa*, meaning "side."
• **Shore** comes from the old German word *schor*, meaning "foreland."
• **Spit** comes from the old English word *spitu*, which in turn comes from the old German word *spizzi*, meaning "pointed."

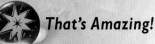
That's Amazing!

At Cape Cod in Massachusetts, U.S.A., about 10,000 waves batter the coast each day, and the cliff retreats landward by 3 feet (1 m) a year. In 1996, the Cape Cod lighthouse, built in 1857, had to be moved 450 feet (137 m) back from the cliff edge to prevent it from falling into the sea.

Pathfinder

• Erosion can change landforms dramatically. Read how on pages 14–15.
• Pebbles and shells that settle on the seafloor may turn into sedimentary rock. Learn how this happens on pages 20–21.
• Beaches provide a wide range of rock samples. Find out how to identify rocks and minerals on pages 54–55.

INSIDE STORY
London Bridge Has Fallen Down

On January 17, 1990, 18-year-old Kelli Harrison and her cousin David Darrington paid a visit to London Bridge, a spectacular double sea arch on the southeast coast of Australia. The cousins had just crossed the bridge when they heard "a huge splash." Looking back, they saw that the ground they had just walked across had vanished. "If we were another 30 seconds later, there is no way in the world we could have survived it," said Kelli. For thousands of years, the waves had been gnawing at the limestone and sandstone cliffs. The arches had stood for centuries, but finally, on this day, one gave way. Thankful to be alive, Kelli and David waited patiently on the new sea stack until a police helicopter carried them to safety.

ON THE BEACH

You'll find rocks of all shapes, colors, and sizes on the seashore. As waves crash into the coast, they grind rocks and pebbles against each other, cracking, smoothing, and polishing them. Over hundreds of years, the water wears the rocks down to sand. If you look at sand under a magnifying glass, you'll see tiny grains of minerals.

Beaches are great places for finding a wide variety of polished pebbles.

Sand dunes form when the wind blows loose, fine sand into large mounds.

At a river mouth, you may find rocks carried from far inland by the river.

Sediments deposited by rivers and waves may trap water, forming a coastal lagoon.

Waves may sculpt rocky terraces at the base of cliffs.

Sand deposited by currents may form a long beach that sticks out into the sea. This is called a spit.

SCANNING THE SHORELINE

As you walk the shore, look for the geological features shown here. At each of these places, you will find different rocks and minerals. Always keep an eye out for big waves and changing tides that may strand you on rocks or beaches.

The nonstop action of the waves digs deeper into the headland. The caves get bigger until they join up. This creates a formation called a sea arch.

Eventually, the top of the arch collapses into the surf, leaving a sea stack. Further stacks may form as the waves continue to pound and pummel the cliffs.

Rhacopteris
plant fossil

Heliobatus
ray fossil

Eucalyptus
plant fossil

Fossil Hunting

ROCKS OFTEN CONTAIN traces of ancient life. These are called fossils. They can be bones, footprints, impressions, or other signs of prehistoric plants or animals. Fossils form when living things walk on or die in swamp, lake, river, or ocean sediments. When the sediments become rock, they may retain the impression of the life form. Sometimes, minerals replace parts of dead animals or plants and turn them into rock.

Hundreds of years ago, people didn't know what to make of fossils. Some thought they were the remains of animals that lived underground. Others believed that fossils grew inside rocks. Today, scientists search for fossils to learn about ancient life forms and environments. The presence of certain fossils can tell us what the climate was like millions of years ago. For example, fossils of coral reefs in the eastern United States suggest that the area was once a tropical sea. Scientists can also use fossils to date rock layers. We know that certain plants and creatures lived at specific times. Their presence or absence can therefore help us work out how old a rock is.

You can be a fossil hunter, too. Look in layers of sedimentary rock, such as sandstone and shale. Limestone often contains fossils of sea creatures. Once you have collected a few fossils, sort them into categories such as vertebrates (animals with backbones), invertebrates (animals with no backbones), and plants. You can put your best samples on display, alongside your rocks and minerals.

PETRIFIED TREES
These stone tree trunks are the remains of ancient trees. They turned to stone when water laden with silica replaced the living tissue with minerals. This process is called petrification.

A GEM OF A FOSSIL
This multicolored shell is a fossil. It formed when water containing silica filled a rock cavity formed by a seashell, or slowly replaced the shell. The silica solution then hardened into opal, a type of gemstone.

INSIDE STORY

She Sells Fossil Shells

At the beginning of the 19th century, scientists had just become aware that fossils were important records of the history of life. Museums and universities began to hunt for and collect fossilized remains of all kinds. In Dorset, England, a girl called Mary Anning helped her father to gather and sell fossilized shells from the local seashore. (It is said that Mary inspired the tongue twister "She sells sea shells by the seashore.") One day in 1811, when Mary was 12, she spotted an unusual, whitish object sticking out

of some rocks. When she carefully chipped away the rock with her hammer, she saw that it was a skeleton. It turned out to be the first complete fossil of an ichthyosaur, a dolphinlike creature that lived between 245 and 65 million years ago. Mary went on to find many other important fossils, some of which are displayed in the British Museum.

PRESERVED IN AMBER
Millions of years ago, this insect was smothered by a glob of sticky tree sap. Slowly, the sap hardened into a substance called amber, which has perfectly preserved this sample of ancient life.

Frozen woolly mammoth

Stegosaurus
skeleton

- **Fossil** comes from the Latin word *fodere*, which means "to dig."
- Scientists who study fossils are called **paleontologists**. This word comes from the Greek *palaios*, meaning "ancient," *onta*, meaning "existing things," and *logos*, meaning "study of."
- **Trilobite** comes from the Greek words *tri*, meaning "three," and *lobos*, meaning "lobe." The name refers to the three parts of the animal's midsection.

- The longest complete dinosaur skeleton comes from remains found in Wyoming, U.S.A., in 1899. *Diplodocus carnegii* measures 87.5 feet (26.6 m) long. That's longer than a tennis court.
- Scientists believe that 99 percent of all the life forms that ever existed on Earth died without leaving any fossil records. Fossilization is truly a special event!

- You are most likely to find fossils in sedimentary rocks. Learn about these rocks on pages 20–21.
- By identifying and dating fossils in rock layers, geologists can reconstruct the history of a landscape. See pages 46–47.
- Coastal cliffs often contain marine fossils. Find out more on pages 56–57.

FROM BONE TO STONE

DIGGING FOR DINOSAURS

These dinosaur bones turned to stone millions of years ago. It happened after the dinosaurs died and their bodies were buried in sediments. Mineral-rich water seeped into the bones, filling the pores with minerals. Today, scientists carefully chisel away the surrounding rock to remove the fossils.

COMMON CRUSTACEANS

Trilobites are among the most common fossils. These crablike sea creatures thrived between 550 and 250 million years ago.

The formation of an animal fossil begins when the creature dies. Its soft body parts decay, leaving the hard parts, such as teeth, bones, or shell.

Gradually, layers of sediments cover the remains. Sometimes, mineral-rich water can seep into the hard body parts and may replace them with minerals.

As the sediments are compacted, they press around the remains. When the sediments turn into rock, the rock retains the imprint of the body parts.

Plate movements bring the fossil to the surface. Erosion may then wear away the rock, revealing more of the fossil.

61

Geologist's microscope

Labradorite: massive habit

Glossary

anticline A fold in layers of sedimentary rock that bulges upward.

asthenosphere A weak layer inside Earth. It is part of the upper mantle and consists of partially molten rock.

atom The smallest unit that can be called a chemical element. All things on Earth are made up of atoms.

bacteria Single-celled, microscopic life-forms found in air, water, plants, animals, and Earth's crust.

butte An obvious, flat-topped, steep-sided hill sometimes found in desert areas. Some form by erosion of a large mesa.

canyon A deep, steep-sided valley formed by river erosion.

clay A fine-grained sediment formed by the chemical breakdown of rocks. It is moldable when wet and hard when dry. It can be baked to make china, pottery, tile, and brick.

coal A sedimentary rock formed by the compression of plant remains and sediment layers. It can be burned for fuel.

compound A chemical substance made up of more than one element. Most minerals are compounds.

concretion A usually rounded, hard mass of mineral matter that typically has a fossil at its core.

contact metamorphism The transformation of one type of rock into another, mostly as a result of heating.

continent One of Earth's seven main landmasses: Africa, Antarctica, Asia, Australia, Europe, North America, and South America. The landmasses include edges beneath the ocean as well as dry land area.

convection currents (mantle) Movement within the mantle caused by heat transfer from Earth's core. Hot rock rises and cooler rock sinks. This movement is most likely responsible for the motion of Earth's tectonic plates.

core The center of Earth. It consists of a solid inner core and a molten outer core, both of which are made of an iron-nickel alloy.

core sample A long column of rock that has been extracted from the ground by drilling with a hollow drill. Geologists use core samples to study rocks, ice, or soil beneath the surface.

crust The outer layer of Earth. There are two types of crust: continental crust, which forms the major landmasses, and oceanic crust, which is thinner and forms the seafloor.

crystal One grain of a mineral. Some crystals have a regular shape with smooth sides.

earthquake A sudden, violent vibration in Earth's crust that generally occurs at the edges of tectonic plates.

element A chemical substance that contains only one kind of atom.

era A division of time in Earth's history. Geologists divide eras into periods.

erosion The gradual wearing away of rock by water, ice, or wind.

evaporation The process by which a liquid turns into a gas without necessarily boiling.

fault A crack in Earth's crust along which motion has occurred.

fluorescent mineral A mineral that glows under ultraviolet light.

fold A bend in layers of rock typically produced when plate movements compress the crust.

fossil Any evidence of pre-existing life. It may be the remains of a plant or animal that have turned to stone or have left their impression in rock.

fossil fuel A fuel that formed when plant remains were compressed under sedimentary rock layers. The most common fossil fuels are coal, oil, and natural gas.

gemstone Any mineral or other natural material that can be cut and polished into a jewel.

geode A rounded, hollow rock that is coated with layers of chalcedony and larger crystals.

geology The study of Earth. Rocks, minerals, and fossils give some of the clues to Earth's history. A person who studies geology is called a geologist.

glacier A large mass of ice formed by the buildup of snow on a mountain or a continent. The ice moves slowly downhill, gouging out rocks and carrying debris.

habit The exterior shape of a single crystal or a group of crystals of the same mineral.

hoodoo A tall column of rock formed by erosion.

hotspot volcano A volcano that forms from a deep plume of magma. It commonly occurs in the middle of a tectonic plate.

igneous rock Rock that forms when magma cools and hardens. Intrusive igneous rock solidifies under ground, and extrusive igneous rock solidifies above ground.

impermeable rock Rock through which liquids cannot pass.

intrusion A large mass of rock that forms under ground when magma is injected into other rocks and then cools and hardens.

Glacier

Hoodoos

kimberlite A type of rock formed from magma in the mantle. It is often associated with diamonds and other minerals from the deep Earth.

lava Magma that has erupted onto Earth's surface.

lithosphere The rigid outer layer of Earth, made up of the crust and the upper mantle.

magma Hot, liquid rock or a mush of liquid rock and crystals found beneath the surface of Earth. When magma erupts onto Earth's surface, it is called lava.

mantle The layer of Earth between the crust and the outer core. It includes the solid lower mantle, the weak asthenosphere, and the solid upper mantle.

massive A manner of occurrence of some minerals in which many mineral grains are intergrown to form a solid mass rather than single crystals with geometric shapes.

mesa A wide, flat-topped hill with steep sides. Small mesas may erode to form buttes.

metal Any of a number of elements that are shiny, moldable, and will conduct electricity. Many metals are found in minerals as compounds.

metamorphic rock Rock formed by the transformation of a pre-existing rock as a result of heat and/or pressure.

meteor A streak of light in the night sky caused by a lump of rock entering Earth's atmosphere from space. Before the rock enters the atmosphere it is known as a meteoroid. If it lands on Earth's surface, it is called a meteorite.

mid-ocean ridge An undersea mountain range formed by magma erupting through the gap between tectonic plates that are moving apart.

mineral A naturally formed solid with an ordered arrangement of atoms found in Earth's crust that is neither plant nor animal.

molecule A cluster of atoms formed when one or more types of atoms join (bond).

native element An element that exists alone and not in combination with another element. Examples include sulfur and gold.

ocean trench A deep and narrow undersea valley formed when the oceanic crust of one tectonic plate collides with the crust of another.

ore A rock or mineral from which it is possible to extract a useful material such as a metal.

ornamental stone A gemstone that is not considered precious but can be used for jewelry or other types of ornamentation.

outcrop The part of a rock formation that is exposed at Earth's surface.

period A standard division of time in Earth's history that is shorter than an era.

petrification The cell-by-cell replacement of organic matter such as bone or wood with minerals from surrounding solutions.

phosphorescent mineral A mineral that continues to glow for a short time after exposure to ultraviolet light.

placer deposits Pieces of heavy minerals found in river or beach sediments. They have been washed away from rocks by flowing water.

plate movement The movement of Earth's tectonic plates, probably caused by convection currents in the mantle.

regional metamorphism Large-scale transformation of one rock type into another as a result of heat and pressure due to plate collisions and the formation of mountains.

rift valley A wide valley formed as a result of the stretching of Earth's crust.

rock A solid mass usually made up of minerals and/or rock fragments.

sedimentary rock Rock formed near Earth's surface from pieces of other rocks or plant or animal remains, or by the buildup of chemical solids.

sediments Weathered pieces of rocks or plant or animal remains that are deposited at the bottom of rivers and lakes by water, wind, or ice.

seismic waves Sound waves that travel through Earth after an earthquake.

solution A mixture of two or more chemical substances. It may be a liquid, a solid, or a gas.

streak test A test that involves rubbing a mineral across an unglazed porcelain tile to produce a powder. The color of the powder left by the mineral can help identify it.

syncline A fold in layers of sedimentary rock that bulges downward.

tectonic plates Rigid pieces of Earth's lithosphere that move over the asthenosphere.

tectonic uplift The raising up of rock as a result of plate movements.

volcanic plug A stump of hard igneous rock that remains after a volcano has been worn away by erosion.

volcano An opening in Earth's crust through which lava erupts. It may form a cone-shaped mountain.

weathering The disintegration of rocks as a result of the freezing and thawing of ice, the action of chemicals in rainwater, or the growth of plant roots.

Index

The publishers would like to thank the following experts and institutions for their assistance in the preparation of this book: Barbara Bakowski, Brian Chase, James Clark, William Henika, Steve Ottinoski, Ross Pogson, Virginia Polytechnic, Dina Rubin, Cynthia Shroba, Ph.D., Jennier Themel. Our special thanks to the following children who feature in the photographs: Michelle Burk, Simon Burk, Elliot Burton, Lisa Chan, Amanda Hanani, Andrew Tout.

PICTURE CREDITS (t=top, b=bottom, l=left, r=right, c=center, e=extreme, f=flap, F=Front, C=Cover, B=Back) (APL=Australian Picture Library, BPK=Bildarchiv Preussischer Kulturbesitz, DWSPL=D.W. Stock Photo Library, FLPA=Frank Lane Picture Agency, NGS=National Geographic Society, NMNH=National Museum of Natural History, Washington, NHM=Natural History Museum, NSP=Natural Science Photos, TPL=The Photo Library, Sydney, SPL=Science Picture Library.)
Ad-Libitum 4tr, 7tr, 8tl, 8tr, 8l, 8bl, 8br, 9bl, 9br, 16c, 19c, 20bl, 20br, 21tl, 22tr, 22bl, 26br, 27cl, 27cr, 28tr, 32/33c, 32bl, 36tl, 36tr, 36bc, 37ct, 37cb, 39t, 41tl, 42b, 47tl, 47tr, 52bl, 54tr, 63br, 35c, 50bl, 50br, 54c, 54br, 55tl, 56bl (M. Kaniewski). **The Age** 59r (S. O'Dwyer). **American Museum of Natural History** 37br, 53br. **APL** 23tl (D&J Heaton), 15b (H. T. Kaiser),13tl (J. Penisten), 15c (S.Vidler). **Association Curie et Joliet-Curie** 50l. **K. Atkinson** 14c. **Auscape** 58r (J. Ferrero), 20r (F. Gohier), 18tr (M & K Krafft), 18/19b (T. Till). **Australian Museum** 53tr, 55r (Nature Focus). **BPK** 45c (Margarete Busing). **The Bridgeman Art Library** 37tr, 44tr. **R. Coenraads** 33br, 35tl, 35tr, 56tr. **Corel Professional Photos** 39br. **DWSPL** 59l (M. Fenech). **The Field Museum, Chicago,** IL. 25br. **FLPA** 23cr (M. Nimmo). **Gannett Suburban Newspapers** 25tr (S. Bayer). **Icelandic Photo** 16tr (Mats Wibe Lund/Sigurg. Jonasson). **Jeff. L. Rottman Photography** 32tl. **Jim Stimson Photography** 22/23c. **The Kobal Collection** 11ct. **Mary Evans Picture Library** 17tr, 32l, 49r, 54bl. **The National Gallery Picture Library, London** 36l. **NASA** 46tr, 46bl. **NGS** 50t (J. L. Amos). **NHM** 25c, 34br, 35br, 60l. **NMNH** 14bl, 28/29c, 38bl (C. Clark), 36/37c. **North Wind Pictures** 21tr, 57tr. **NSP** 30tr (O. C. Roura). **TPL** 21r (O. Benn), 60tr (S. Fraser), 46br (G.B. Lewis), 47br (Dr. K Macdonald), 39b (NASA), 52tr (P. Hayson), 49c (A. Husmo), 42c (P. Robinson), 10t, 12tr (SPL), 48bl (SPL/C. Caffrey), 11cb (SPL/ Geoscape). **Photo Researchers Inc.** 28l (T. McHugh),

20/21c (C. Ott), 29br (G. Retherford). **Planet Earth Pictures** 24tr (E. Darack). **G.R "Dick" Roberts** 30l. **Scottish National Portrait Gallery** 23tr. **J. Scovil** 24l, 24br, 29c, 30cr, 30br, 31l, 31r, 32t, 33t, 34l, 38c, 38cr, 39tl, 39cl, 39bl, 60br. **B. Shelton** 60cr. **Tiffany & Co.** 34tr. **Tom Stack & Associates** 17br. **Tom Till Photography** 19t. **Visuals Unlimited** 44c (J. Greenberg), 57br (D. Thomas). **Werner Forum Archive** 18bl. **William Mallat Photography** 51bl.

ILLUSTRATION CREDITS
Susanna Addario 4cr, 5tr, 6br, 12tl, 14tl, 32tc, 39r, 40tcr, 42tr, 44tl, 44tc, 63tr. **Andrew Beckett/illustration** 8/9c, 6tr. **Anne Bowman** 41bl, 41br, 60tl, 60tc, 60tr, 61tl. **Chris Forsey** 4br, 6tcr, 6bcr, 10/11c, 10t, 10/11b, 11r, 12/13c, 14/15c, 14bl, 15r, 16/17c, 16/17b, 40cr, 40bcr, 41cr, 46/47c, 46tl, 46tc, 46b, 47bl, 48/49c, 48tl, 48tc, 48tr, 48bl, 48br, 49bl, 49br, 58/59c, 58tl, 58tc, 58tr, 58etr, 58br, 59bl, 59br, 62tl, 62bc, 62br. **Ray Grinaway** 7tl, 7cl, 7cr, 7br, 10bl, 18tl, 18bl, 18br, 19tl, 20tl, 20tc, 20tr, 22tl, 22tc, 22tr, 24tl, 24tc, 24tr, 25tl, 26tl, 26tr, 26cr, 26bcr, 27tl, 27bl, 28tl, 28tc, 28tr, 28b, 29tr, 29b, 30tl, 30tc, 30tr, 30bl, 30br, 31cr, 31bl, 31bc, 31br, 32tr, 33r, 34tl, 34tc, 36bl, 36br, 37bl, 37br, 37c, 38tl, 38tc, 38bl, 39tr, 39cr, 39r, 41tr, 45tr, 45tc, 54tl, 54tc, 54tr, 55r, 55b, 60br, 61c, 62tc, 62tr, 63tr, 63bc. **Frank Knight** 60bl. **David McAllister** 42bl, 42br, 43c, 43bl, 43br. **Stuart McVicar** (digital manipulation)13tr. **Oliver Rennert** 12tr. **Claudia Saracini** 16tc. **Michael Saunders** 14tc, 14tr, 14b, 16tr, 19tr, 19cr, 19br, 20br, 21bl, 21br, 22/23b, 24br, 25bl, 25br, 27tr, 34tr, 34b, 35bl, 35br, 39r, 40tr, 41cl, 42tl, 42tc, 42r, 44tr, 56/57c, 56tl, 56tc, 56tr, 56b, 57bl, 57br, 61r, 62bl, 63tc, 63tr. **Kevin Stead** 27br, 38tr. **Sharif Tarabay/illustration** 52/53c, 52/53b, 52cl, 52tc, 52tcr, 52tcr. **S. Trevaskis** 44bl. **Thomas Trojer** 39c, 40br, 50/51c, 50tl, 50tc, 50tr, 51r. **Rod Westblade** 12tc. **Ann Winterbotham** 16tl.

COVER CREDITS
Susanna Addario Bfbr, BCetr, BCtr, BCetl, Bildarchiv Preussischer Kulturbesitz FCbr (Margarete Busing), **Anne Bowman** FCetr, **Chris Forsey** Bftl, Bftr, Bfbl, BCb, Ffc, Ffb, **Ray Grinaway** Bfebr, BCebl, BCebc, BCebl, BCtl, BCcl, FCtl, FCl, FCtr FCcr, **Photo Researchers Inc.** FCc (T. McHugh), **Michael Saunders** BCbr, BCbl, FCr, Fft, **Kevin Stead** FCtc, **Sharif Tarabay/illustration** Bfc, **Ann Winterbotham** BCc.